CELTIC VERSE

CELTIC

VERSE

AN INSPIRATIONAL ANTHOLOGY OF PROSE, POEMS, PRAYERS AND WORDS OF WISDOM

EDITED BY
Elaine Gill and David Everett

BLANDFORD

A Blandford Book

First published in the UK 1998 by Blandford
a Cassell imprint

Cassell plc
Wellington House
125 Strand
London WC2R 0BB

Introduction, selection and editorial matter
© 1998
Elaine Gill and David Everett

Distributed in the United States by
Sterling Publishing Co., Inc.,
387 Park Avenue South, New York,
NY 10016-8810

A Cataloguing-in-Publication Data entry for
this title is available from the British Library

ISBN 0-7137-2616-4

Designed by Harry Green
Printed and bound in England
by Mackays of Chatham

CONTENTS

INTRODUCTION

The pieces for this anthology of Celtic verse and prose have been chosen rather like a wandering goat browsing and nibbling as it goes, taking a tasty morsel from this bush and a mouthful from that. It is certainly not a comprehensive overview of Celtic literature from the earliest manuscripts to the most contemporary of works, although it includes both translations of early texts and also modern poems. It is a selection to give a taste. We make no apology for this, but hope you will enjoy the wide sweep and rejoice in the range and diversity of the material. Some things have been included simply because we like them!

Most of the authors and poets are 'Celtic' by birth or family, that is they hail from those places considered by people today to be the Celtic nations. But some, like Francis Kilvert, have long been associated with a Celtic landscape and have captured something of the distinctiveness that marks out and sets apart these lands.

The themes of the sections are universal ones, not unique to the Celtic peoples but explored by the poets and authors from a Celtic perspective; thus they take on a characteristic colour and express a particular outlook. Some pieces could have been included in several of the categories, and in some cases the decision to place them where we have has been somewhat arbitrary. However, we hope that there is a Celtic thread running through the book which gives a unified feeling to the chosen material, and that the poignancy and passion of life and death perceived and experienced by the Celts comes through these pages.

ELAINE GILL   DAVID EVERETT
Penzance   Camborne

Cornwall/Kernow, 1997

ACKNOWLEDGEMENTS

The compilers and publishers gratefully acknowledge permission to reproduce the following copyright material in this book. Every effort has been made to trace copyright owners, and the compilers and publishers apologize to anyone whose rights have inadvertently not been acknowledged. This will be corrected in any reprint.

DAFYDD AP GWILYM: 'May and January', 'The Seagull', 'The Mist', translated by R.M. Loomis, © R.M. Loomis 1982. Reprinted by permission of the Center for Medieval and Early Renaissance Studies, Binghamton, USA.

RUTH BIDGOOD: 'At Nevern', 'At Strata Florida', 'Burial Path' from *Selected Poems*, © Ruth Bidgood 1992. Reprinted by permission of Seren.

GEORGE MACKAY BROWN: 'Kirkyard' from *Selected Poems, 1954–1983*, © George Mackay Brown 1991. Reprinted by permission of John Murray (Publishers) Ltd.

ALEXANDER CARMICHAEL: 'Thou Great Lord of the Sun', extract from *Carmina Gadelica*, © Scottish Academic Press 1941. Reprinted by permission of the Trustees of the Scottish Academic Press.

IAIN CRICHTON SMITH: 'Johnson in the Highlands', from *Collected Poems*, © Iain Crichton Smith 1986. Reprinted by permission of Carcanet Press Ltd.

PADRAIC COLUM: 'She Moved Through the Fair', © Padraic Colum 1981. Reprinted by permission of Maire Colum O'Sullivan.

EXTRACT FROM 'DRUIDIC TRIADS', © Sure Fire Press 1984. Reprinted by permission of Sure Fire Press, Holman Publishing Group.

W.S. GRAHAM: 'Pangur', © The estate of W.S. Graham 1993. Reprinted by permission of Mrs W.S. Graham.

JOHN HARRIS: 'The Mine', © Paul Newman 1994 Reprinted by permission of Dyllansow Truran.

SEAMUS HEANEY: 'St Kevin and the Blackbird', from *The Spirit Level*, © Seamus Heaney 1996. Reprinted by permission of Faber and Faber.

K.H. JACKSON: 'I Have Tidings for You', 'A Good Tranquil Season is Autumn', 'Usual is Wind from the South', extract from 'The Life of Ciaran of Saighir' from *Early Celtic Nature Poetry*, © K.H. Jackson 1935. Reprinted by permission of Cambridge

University Press. 'The Hermit's Hut', 'St Columba's Island Hermitage', 'The Blackthorn Pin', 'He Whose Hand and Eye are Gentle', extract from 'The Voyage of Mael Dúin' from *A Celtic Miscellany*, © K.H. Jackson 1951. Reprinted by permission of Routledge.

FRANCIS KILVERT: Extract from *Kilvert's Diary 1870–79*, © Mrs Sheila Hooper. Reprinted by permission of Jonathan Cape.

THOMAS KINSELLA: Extracts from 'The Tain', © Thomas Kinsella 1969. Reprinted by permission of Thomas Kinsella.

ALUN LEWIS: 'The Mountain Over Aberdare', 'The Rhondda' from *Collected Poems*, © Alun Lewis 1994. Reprinted by permission of Seren.

CARL LOFMARK: 'Song of the Old Man', 'Elergy for Llewelyn ap Gruffydd', © Carl Lofmark 1989. Reprinted by permission of Llanerch Press.

DONNELLY MCCORMICK: 'Wear Those Lovely Colours For Me', © Donnelly McCormick 1996. Printed by permission of the author.

HUGH MACDIARMID: 'The Little White Rose', from *Complete Poems*, © Hugh MacDiarmid 1934. Reprinted by permission of Carcanet Press Ltd.

ALISDAIR MACLEAN: 'Death of an Old Woman' from *From the Wilderness*, © Alisdair MacLean 1973. Reprinted by permission of Victor Gollancz.

SORLEY MACLEAN: 'Highland Woman', from *From Wood to Ridge*, © Sorley Maclean 1989. Reprinted by permission of Carcarnet Press Ltd.

JAMES MACPHERSON: Extracts from 'The Six Bards', extracts from 'Connal', from *Fragments of Ancient Poetry*, © James MacPherson 1994. Reprinted by permission of Carcanet Press Ltd.

MEIRION PENNAR: 'Maytime Thoughts' translated from the Welsh by Meirion Pennar, © Meirion Pennar 1989. Reprinted by permission of Llanerch Press.

SHEENAGH PUGH: 'King Billy on the Walls', from *Selected Poems*, © Sheenagh Pugh 1990. Reprinted by permission of Seren.

E.D. SEDDING: 'An Iona Benedicite', © E.D. Sedding SSJE. Reprinted by permission of the Society of St John the Evangelist.

R.J. STEWART: Extract from 'Walker Between Worlds', an edition of *The Secret Commonwealth of Elves, Fauns and Fairies* by Robert Kirk. Reprinted by permission of Element Books, Shaftesbury, UK, 1990.

DYLAN THOMAS: 'Fern Hill', from *Collected Poems 1934–52*; extract from 'A Child's Christmas in Wales', © Dylan Thomas 1952. Reprinted by permission of David Higham Associates.

R.S. THOMAS: 'A Peasant', 'The Chapel' and 'The Bright Field', from *Collected Poems 1945–1990*, © R.S. Thomas. Reprinted by permission of J.M. Dent.

W.B. YEATS: 'At Galway Races', 'Down by the Salley Gardens', 'The Stolen Child', 'The Valley of the Black Pig', from *The Collected Poems of W.B. Yeats*. Reprinted by permission of A.P. Watt Ltd on behalf of Michael Yeats.

PLACES

COME BY THE HILLS

In recent years our new awareness of ecological issues has given us the idea of the earth as a living being. Celtic people are rooted in the land and are still conscious of this ancient connection. Their lives are bound up with their landscape, whether it is the beauty and grandeur of mountains or sea-cliffs or the bleakness of 'the rough foreheads of these moody hills' or 'derelict workings, tips of slag'.

Often this sense of place is infused with the numinous where the poet tells how Saint 'Brynach walked with angels' or how the lost lands of Kaer-Is can be dreamed of.

Whatever the landscape, one can never be indifferent; an emotional response is demanded in these dramatic places 'where legend remains' and where poetry is 'in the pebbles of the holy streams'.

The Hermit's Hut

...I have a hut in the wood, none knows it but my Lord; an ash tree this side, a hazel on the other, a great tree on a mound encloses it.

Two heathery door-posts for support, and a lintel of honey-suckle; around its close the wood sheds its nuts upon fat swine.

The size of my hut, small yet not small, a place of familiar paths; the she-bird in its dress of blackbird colour sings a melodious strain from its gable.

The stags of Druim Rolach leap out of its stream of trim meadows; from them red Roighne can be seen, noble Mucraimhe and Maenmhagh.

A little hidden lowly hut, which owns the path-filled forest; will you go with me to see it?...

A tree of apples of great bounty,..., huge; a seemly crop from small-nutted branching green hazels, in clusters like a fist.

Excellent fresh springs – a cup of water, splendid to drink – they gush forth abundantly; yew berries, bird-cherries...

Tame swine lie down around it, goats, young pigs, wild swine, tall deer, does, a badger's brood.

Peaceful, in crowds, a grave host of the countryside, an assembly at my house; foxes come to the wood before it – it is delightful...

Fruits of rowan, black sloes of the dark blackthorn; foods of whorts, spare berries...

A clutch of eggs, honey, produce of heath-peas, God has sent it; sweet apples, red bog-berries, whortleberries.

Beer with herbs, a patch of strawberries, delicious abundance; haws, yew berries, kernels of nuts.

A cup of mead from the goodly hazel-bush, quickly served; brown acorns, manes of briar, with fine blackberries.

In summer with its pleasant, abundant mantle, with good-tasting savour, there are pignuts, wild marjoram, the cresses of the stream – green purity!

The songs of the bright-breasted ring-doves, a beloved movement, the carol of the thrush, pleasant and familiar above my house.

Swarms of bees, beetles, soft music of the world, a gentle humming; wild geese, barnacle geese, shortly before All Hallows, music of the dark torrent.

A nimble singer, the combative brown wren from the hazel bough, woodpeckers with their pied hoods in a vast host.

Fair white birds come, cranes, seagulls, the sea sings to them, no mournful music; brown fowl out of the red heather.

The heifer is noisy in summer, brightest of weather; not bitter or toilsome over the mellow plain, delightful, smooth.

The voice of the wind against the branchy wood, grey with cloud; cascades of the river, the swan's song, lovely music.

A beautiful pine makes music to me, it is not hired; through Christ, I fare no worse at any time than you do.

Though you delight in your own enjoyments, greater than all wealth, for my part I am grateful for what is given me from my dear Christ.

Without an hour of quarrel, without the noise of strife which disturbs you, grateful to the Prince who gives every good to me in my hut...

IRISH (10th century)

translated by K.H. JACKSON

At Nevern

Nevern, signed with David's cross and Brynach's,
lay hushed and innocent. We stood
in the sunny churchyard. Tower and trees
rippled with heat-haze, as if a tiny breeze
passed over baptismal water
in a golden font. On Carn Ingli above,
Brynach walked with angels; the afternoon
was a pause in their conversation.
Silence surrounded the laughter of children
who broke from yew-trees' shadow
to run between the tombs.
Perception reached out to the hills
tentatively as a hand
to a loved face. Unborn words
were given into winged keeping.
In dusk on the northward road
we were too far away to hear
when at the carn the voices began again.

RUTH BIDGOOD (b. 1922)

from Kilvert's Diary 1870–1879

Friday, 22 July, 1870

At last we got off and drove to Kynance Cove. The carriage was left on the moors (or 'Croft' as it is called here) above, and we scrambled down into the Cove. The tide was ebbing fast and it was nearly low water. We wandered about through the Dining Room and Drawing Room Caves, and among the huge Serpentine Cliffs and the vast detached rocks which stand like giants guarding the Cove. I never saw anything like the wonderful colour of the serpentine rocks, rich, deep, warm, variegated, mottled and streaked and veined with red, green and white, huge blocks and masses of precious stone marble on every side, an enchanted cove, the palace of the Nereids.

In one of the Serpentine shops at the Lizard there was a stuffed Cornish Chough. He is an elegantly shaped black bird cleanly made with red or orange beak and legs. He is very rarely found now even along the Cornish Cliffs.

Friday, 29 July, 1870

Then we came to Zennor, the strange old tower in the granite wilderness in a hollow of the wild hillside, a corner and end of the world, desolate, solitary, bare, dreary, the cluster of white and grey houses round the massive old granite Church tower, a sort of place that might have been quite lately discovered and where 'fragments of forgotten peoples might dwell'.

FRANCIS KILVERT (1840–79)

The Drowning of Kaer-Is

I

Heard ye the word the man of God
Spake to King Gradlon, blythe of mood,
Where in fair Kaer-Is he abode?

"Sir King, of dalliance be not fain,
From evil loves thy heart refrain,
For hard on pleasure followeth pain.

"Who feeds his fill on fish of sea
To feed the fishes doom'd is he;
The swallower swallow'd up shall be.

"Who drinks of the wine and the barley-brew,
Of water shall drink as the fishes do;–
Who knows not this shall learn 'tis true."

II

Unto his guests King Gradlon said,
"My merry feres, the day is sped;
I will betake me to my bed.

"Drink on, drink on, till morning light,
In feast and dalliance waste the night;
For all that will the board is dight."

To Gradlon's daughter, bright of blee,
Her lover he whisper'd, tenderly:
"Bethink thee, sweet Dahut, the key!"

"Oh! I'll win the key from my father's side,
That bolts the sluice and bars the tide;
To work thy will is thy lady's pride."

III

Whoso that ancient king had seen,
Asleep in his bed of the golden sheen,
Dumb-stricken all for awe had been –

To see him laid in his robe of grain,
His hair like snow, on his white hause-bane,
And round his neck his golden chain.

Whoso had watch'd that night, I weet,
Had seen a maiden stilly fleet
In at the door, on naked feet,

To the old King's side, she hath stolen free,
And hath kneeled her down upon her knee,
And lightly hath ta'en both chain and key.

IV

He sleepeth still, he sleepeth sound,
When, hark, a cry from the lower ground –
"The sluice is oped, Kaer-Is is drown'd!

"Awake, Sir King, the gates unspar!
Rise up, and ride both fast and far!
The sea flows over bolt and bar!"

Now cursèd for ever mote she be,
That all for wine and harlotry,
The sluice unbarr'd that held the sea!

V

"Say, woodman, that wonn'st in the forest green,
The wild horse of Gradlon hast thou seen,
As he pass'd the valley-walls between?"

"On Gradlon's horse I set not sight,
But I heard him go by in the dark of night,
Trip, trep, – trip, trep, – like a fire-flaught white!"

"Say, fisher, the mermaid hast thou seen,
Combing her hair by the sea-waves green –
Her hair like gold in the sunlight sheen?"

"I saw the white maiden of the sea,
And I heard her chaunt her melody,
And her song was sad as the wild waves be."

BRETON (19th century)
translated by TOM TAYLOR

18

St Columba's Island Hermitage

Delightful I think it to be in the bosom of an isle, on the peak of a rock, that I might often see there the calm of the sea.

That I might see its heavy waves over the glittering ocean, as they chant a melody to their Father on their eternal course.

That I might see its smooth strand of clear headlands, no gloomy thing; that I might hear the voice of the wondrous birds, a joyful tune.

That I might hear the sound of the shallow waves against the rocks; that I might hear the cry by the graveyard, the noise of the sea.

That I might see its splendid flocks of birds over the full-watered ocean; that I might see its mighty whales, greatest of wonders.

That I might see its ebb and its flood-tide in their flow; that this might be my name, a secret I tell, 'He who turned his back on Ireland.'

That contrition of heart should come upon me as I watch it; that I might bewail my many sins, difficult to declare.

That I might bless the Lord who has power over all, Heaven with its pure host of angels, earth, ebb, flood-tide.

That I might pore on one of my books, good for my soul; a while kneeling for beloved Heaven, a while at psalms.

A while gathering dulse from the rock, a while fishing, a while giving food to the poor, a while in my cell.

A while meditating upon the Kingdom of Heaven, holy is the redemption; a while at labour not too heavy; it would be delightful!

IRISH (12th century)

translated by K.H. JACKSON

Fern Hill

Now as I was young and easy under the apple boughs
About the lilting house and happy as the grass was green,
  The night above the dingle starry,
   Time let me hail and climb
  Golden in the heydays of his eyes,
And honoured among wagons I was prince of the apple towns
And once below a time I lordly had the trees and leaves
   Trail with daisies and barley
  Down the rivers of the windfall light.

And as I was green and carefree, famous among the barns
About the happy yard and singing as the farm was home,
  In the sun that is young once only,
   Time let me play and be
  Golden in the mercy of his means,
And green and golden I was huntsman and herdsman, the calves
Sang to my horn, the foxes on the hills barked clear and cold,
   And the sabbath rang slowly
  In the pebbles of the holy streams.

All the sun long it was running, it was lovely, the hay
Fields high as the house, the tunes from the chimneys, it was air
  And playing, lovely and watery
   And fire green as grass.
  And nightly under the simple stars
As I rode to sleep the owls were bearing the farm away,
All the moon long I heard, blessed among stables, the nightjars
  Flying with the ricks, and the horses
   Flashing into the dark.

And then to awake, and the farm, like a wanderer white
With the dew, come back, the cock on his shoulder: it was all
  Shining, it was Adam and maiden,
   The sky gathered again
  And the sun grew round that very day.

So it must have been after the birth of the simple light
In the first, spinning place, the spellbound horses walking warm
    Out of the whinnying green stable
        On to the fields of praise.

And honoured among foxes and pheasants by the gay house
Under the new made clouds and happy as the heart was long,
    In the sun born over and over,
        I ran my heedless ways,
    My wishes raced through the house high hay
And nothing I cared, at my sky blue trades, that time allows
In all his tuneful turning so few and such morning songs
    Before the children green and golden
        Follow him out of grace,

Nothing I cared, in the lamb white days, that time would take me
Up to the swallow thronged loft by the shadow of my hand,
    In the moon that is always rising,
        Nor that riding to sleep
    I should hear him fly with the high fields
And wake to the farm forever fled from the childless land.
Oh as I was young and easy in the mercy of his means,
        Time held me green and dying
    Though I sang in my chains like the sea.

DYLAN THOMAS (1914–53)

The Emigrant's Departure

He stood upon his native mount,
    And gazed upon the sky:
'T was bluer than 't was wont to be,
    Or *look'd* so to his eye.
And when the evening sun went down
    Behind the wavy west,
The tear-drop glisten'd in his eye,
    And heaved his labouring breast.

The music of the evening bells
    Came on the harping breeze;
And O how sweet, how passing sweet,
    It floated through the trees!
Dame Nature tuned her sweetest lyre,
    Or *seem'd* to tune it, then:
He never heard such melody,
    Nor hoped to hear again!

The peasants in the vale below
    Were at their evening meal;
And when the merry village hum
    Did o'er his senses steal,
He turned away his aching eye
    From scenes so dear beneath,
And dropp'd a tear in solitude
    Upon the rustling heath.

O! there were notes too sweet to last,
    That swept across the plain;
And there were shadows of the past,
    That flash'd across his brain:
And there were in his watery eye,
    Around him and above,
In every corner of the sky,
    Sweet images of love!

He thought the first bright flowers of May
　　Had never look'd so fair,
As when his last long lingering glance
　　He bent upon them there.
He kiss'd the little murmuring stream
　　Within his native dell,
And, as the evening star came forth,
　　He sigh'd his last farewell!

The moon arose, and shower'd her beams
　　Upon the ivied rocks,
And twined her silver tissues with
　　The mountain's heather-locks;
When, with his hawthorn staff in hand,
　　He left his cottage-door,
And wander'd to a foreign land,
　　And here was seen no more.

JOHN HARRIS (1820–84)

The Mountain Over Aberdare

From this high quarried ledge I see
The place for which the Quakers once
Collected clothes, my fathers' home,
Our stubborn bankrupt village sprawled
In jaded dusk beneath its nameless hills;
The drab streets strung across the cwm,
Derelict workings, tips of slag
The gospellers and gamblers use
And children scrutting for the coal
That winter dole cannot purvey;
Allotments where the collier digs
While engines hack the coal within his brain;
Grey Hebron in a rigid cramp,
White cheap-jack cinema, the church
Stretched like a sow beside the stream;
And mourners in their Sunday best
Holding a tiny funeral, singing hymns
That drift insidious as the rain
Which rises from the steaming fields
And swathes about the skyline crags
Till all the upland gorse is drenched
And all the creaking mountain gates
Drip brittle tears of crystal peace;
And in a curtained parlour women hug
Huge grief, and anger against God.

But now the dusk, more charitable than Quakers,
Veils the cracked cottages with drifting may
And rubs the hard day off the slate.
The colliers squatting on the ashtip
Listen to one who holds them still with tales,
While that white frock that floats down the dark alley
Looks just like Christ; and in the lane
The clink of coins among the gamblers
Suggests the thirty pieces of silver.
I watch the clouded years
Rune the rough foreheads of these moody hills,
This wet evening, in a lost age.

ALUN LEWIS (1915–44)

Come By The Hills

Come by the hills to the land
    where fancy is free.
And stand where the peaks meet the sky
    and the rocks reach the sea.
Where the rivers run clear and the bracken
    is gold in the sun,
And cares of tomorrow must wait
    till this day is done.

Come by the hills to the land
    where life is a song
And sing while the birds fill the air
    with their joy all day long.
Where the trees sway in time, and even
    the wind sings in tune,
And cares of tomorrow must wait
    till this day is done.

Come by the hills to the land
    where legend remains
Where stories of old stir the heart
    and may yet come again.
Where the past has been lost and the future
    is still to be won,
And cares of tomorrow must wait
    till this day is done.

Come by the hills to the land
    where fancy is free
And stand where the peaks meet the sky
    and the rocks reach the sea.
Where the rivers run clear and the bracken
    is gold in the sun,
And cares of tomorrow must wait
    till this day is done.

TRADITIONAL IRISH

from The Life of Samuel Johnson

His "Journey to the Western Islands of Scotland" is a most valuable performance. It abounds in extensive philosophical views of society, and in ingenious sentiment and lively description. A considerable part of it, indeed, consists of speculations, which, many years before he saw the wild regions which we visited together, probably had employed his attention, though the actual sight of those scenes undoubtedly quickened and augmented them. Mr. Orme, the very able historian, agreed with me in this opinion, which he thus strongly expressed:– "There are in that book thoughts, which, by long revolution in the great mind of Johnson, have been formed and polished like pebbles rolled in the ocean!"

That he was to some degree of excess a *true-born Englishman*, so as to have entertained an undue prejudice against both the country and the people of Scotland, must be allowed. But it was a prejudice of the head, and not of the heart. He had no ill will to the Scotch; for, if he had been conscious of that, he never would have thrown himself into the bosom of their country, and trusted to the protection of its remote inhabitants with a fearless confidence. His remark upon the nakedness of the country, from its being denuded of trees, was made after having travelled two hundred miles along the Eastern coast, where certainly trees are not to be found near the road; and he said it was "a map of the road" which he gave.

JAMES BOSWELL (1740–95)

Johnson in the Highlands

A reasoning mind travels through this country.
In these sad wastes a Londoner by choice
sees water falling, and some meagre deer.

Examines with his tough reasoning mind
lochs, deer, and people: is not seduced
by Mrs Radcliffe's green hysteria

from a musical prose we've never once achieved,
whose fences cannot reach between the words
whose arguments are broken-backed with exile.

A classical sanity considers Skye.
A huge hard light falls across shifting hills.
This mind, contemptuous of miracles

and beggarly sentiment, illuminates
a healthy moderation. But I hear
like a native dog notes beyond his range

the modulations of a queer music
twisting his huge black body in the pain
that shook him also in raw blazing London.

IAIN CRICHTON SMITH (b. 1928)

Holyhead. Sept. 25, 1727

Lo here I sit at Holyhead
With muddy ale and mouldy bread
All Christian victuals stink of fish
I'm where my enemies would wish
Convict of lies is every sign,
The inn has not one drop of wine
I'm fasten'd both by wind and tide
I see the ship at anchor ride
The Captain swears the sea's too rough
He has not passengers enough.
And thus the Dean is forc'd to stay
Till others come to help the pay
In Dublin they'd be glad to see
A packet though it brings in me.
They cannot say the winds are cross
Your politicians at a loss
For want of matter swears and frets,
Are forced to read the old gazettes.
I never was in haste before
To reach that slavish hateful shore
Before, I always found the wind
To me was most malicious kind
But now, the danger of a friend
On whom my fears and hopes depend
Absent from whom all climes are curst
With whom I'm happy in the worst
With rage impatient makes me wait
A passage to the land I hate.
Else, rather on this bleaky shore
Where loudest winds incessant roar
Where neither herb nor tree will thrive,
Where nature hardly seems alive,
I'd go in freedom to my grave,
Than rule yon isle and be a slave.

JONATHAN SWIFT (1667–1745)

PEOPLE
HEARERS AND HEARTENERS

The interconnectedness of people with the land was mentioned in the previous section, and it was out of this relationship that the songs and poetry grew, moulded by the soil.

The Celts were tribal and had a strong sense of community. This didn't mean that they were dull and uninteresting. Rather it fostered an environment where characters with highly individual traits could flourish and be appreciated. The peasant, the old man or woman, each had a life of their own and a story to tell; a dignity and a value was accorded them and their contribution to that community was recognized and acknowledged.

Gerald of Wales writing in the late twelfth century about Welsh song observes 'you will hear as many different parts and voices as you see heads: but in the end they all join together in a smooth and sweet … resonance and melodic harmony'. The singing was, and still is, a means of expressing the unity and diversity within their society.

At Galway Races

There where the course is,
Delight makes all of the one mind,
The riders upon the galloping horses,
The crowd that closes in behind:
We, too, had good attendance once,
Hearers and hearteners of the work;
Aye, horsemen for companions,
Before the merchant and the clerk
Breathed on the world with timid breath.
Sing on: somewhere at some new moon,
We'll learn that sleeping is not death,
Hearing the whole earth change its tune,
Its flesh being wild, and it again
Crying aloud as the racecourse is,
And we find hearteners among men
That ride upon horses.

W.B. YEATS (1865–1939)

from Description of Wales

They do not live in towns, villages, or castles,
but cling to the woods like hermits. It is their
custom to raise on the edge of woods not great,
high palaces or sumptuous and superfluous
buildings of stone and mortar, but wattle huts,
sufficient for one year's use, involving only
moderate effort and cost.

… the Welsh do not sing their traditional songs
in unison, but in many parts, and in many
modes and modulations. So that in a choir of
singers – a customary thing among these
people – you will hear as many different parts
and voices as you see heads: but in the end
they all join together in a smooth and sweet
B-flat resonance and melodic harmony.

GERALD OF WALES (c.1145–1223)

A Highland Woman

Hast Thou seen her, great Jew,
who art called the One Son of God?
Hast Thou seen on Thy way the like of her
labouring in the distant vineyard?

The load of fruits on her back,
a bitter sweat on brow and cheek,
and the clay basin heavy on the back
of her bent poor wretched head.

Thou hast not seen her, Son of the carpenter,
who art called the King of Glory,
among the rugged western shores
in the sweat of her food's creel.

This Spring and last Spring
and every twenty Springs from the beginning,
she has carried the cold seaweed
for her children's food and the castle's reward.

And every twenty Autumns gone
she has lost the golden summer of her bloom,
and the Black Labour has ploughed the furrow
across the white smoothness of her forehead.

And Thy gentle church has spoken
about the lost state of her miserable soul,
and the unremitting toil has lowered
her body to a black peace in a grave.

And her time has gone like a black sludge
seeping through the thatch of a poor dwelling:
and hard Black Labour was her inheritance;
grey is her sleep to-night.

SORLEY MACLEAN (1911–96)

Song of the Old Man

Before I grew crooked of back, I was
    skilful with words.
My exploits were famed.
The men of Argoed were always
    behind me.

Before I grew crooked of back,
    I was bold.
I was welcome in the mead-halls
Of Powys, paradise of Wales.

Before I grew crooked of back, I was
    magnificent.
My spear was the first to draw blood.
Now I am bent. I am weary. I am
    pitiful.

Wooden staff, it is autumn.
Red-brown the bracken, yellow
    the stubble.
I have lost that which I love.

Wooden staff, it is winter.
Men talk wildly at their drink.
Nobody comes to my bedside.

Wooden staff, it is springtime.
Red-brown the cuckoos; the
    sunshine is bright.
No maiden loves me.

Wooden staff, summer is near.
Red-brown is the furrow; the first
    corn is curly.
With grief I look at your crook.

Wooden staff, knotty branch,
Support a sad old man,
Llywarch, who mutters to himself.

Wooden staff, hard branch,
May God preserve you.
My trusty stick I call you.

Wooden staff, be faithful.
Support me better than before,
For I am Llywarch, always
    muttering.

There is mockery for age,
Upon me, my hair and my teeth,
And the tool which young folk love.

For age there is mockery,
Upon me, my hair and my teeth,
And the tool which women love.

Strong is the wind; white is the edge
    of the wood.
Bold the stag, barren the hill.
Weak the old man, slow to move.

This leaf, driven by the wind,
Sad is her fate.
She is old, though this year born.

What I loved as a boy is now hateful
    to me:
A maiden, a stranger, a spirited
    horse.
They do not suit me now.

Always I hated four things most:
Now they have met in me together.
Coughing, old age, sickness, sorrow.

I am old and alone, mis-shapen,
    cold.
After an honourable bed
I am pitiful, I am three times bent.

I am bent and old, perverse and
    awkward.
I am foolish, I am argumentative.
Those who once loved me love me
    no more.

The girls do not love me; nobody
    visits me.
I cannot move myself about.
Why does death not come to me?

Sleep and joy do not visit me
Since Llawr and Gwên were slain.
I am an irritable corpse. I am old.

Sad was the fate that was fated for
    Llywarch
Since the night when he was born.
Long hardship without release.

WELSH (9th century)

from The Festival of Lughnasa

"As I remember it, I heard the old people say that it was on the first Sunday of the month of Lughnasa they used to have a great day on the tops of the hills about here looking for bilberries. This Sunday was set out specially for the young people to go off to the hills as soon as the mid-day meal was eaten and they would not return again until twilight had fallen... Those nearer Beltany went to the top of that hill and in the same way people living near Carn Treuna went there. Indeed the young boys used to go to whichever place their girls would be...

"After reaching the top of the hill they would sit and eat their lunches. They used to bring flat cakes of oatmeal and milk for the day. Then they would go here and there over the hill looking for bilberries. Sometimes they would scatter in pairs – boys and girls – and other times they would go in groups...

"When they returned from their gathering of bilberries they had a strange custom. They all sat down on the hill-top and the boys began to make bracelets of bilberries for the girls. They had brought short threads in their pockets for the purpose... Each man would then compete with another as to which would make the best and prettiest bracelet for his own girl. When that was done, a man or maybe a girl would be named to sing a song. The melody would begin then and would go round from one to another, and anyone who had a note of music at all in his head would have to keep the fun going.

"After the singing they would begin the dancing. According to the old talk, they had no instrument for music at all; they had to make do with lilting. In those days boys and girls were good at lilting and they would make enough music for those who were dancing…

"When all was over then and they were preparing to go home, the girls would take off the bilberry bracelets and leave them on the hill-top. Whatever meaning there was to that, none of the old people were able to tell me, but they all knew it and they heard from their elders that it was customary for them to do that. They would all come down then and go home."

ORAL ACCOUNT FROM CO. DONEGAL (1942)
translated by MÁIRE MACNEILL

A Peasant

Iago Prytherch his name, though, be it allowed,
Just an ordinary man of the bald Welsh hills,
Who pens a few sheep in a gap of cloud.
Docking mangels, chipping the green skin
From the yellow bones with a half-witted grin
Of satisfaction, or churning the crude earth
To a stiff sea of clouds that glint in the wind –
So are his days spent, his spittled mirth
Rarer than the sun that cracks the cheeks
Of the gaunt sky perhaps once in a week.
And then at night see him fixed in his chair
Motionless, except when he leans to gob in the fire.
There is something frightening in the vacancy of his mind.
His clothes, sour with years of sweat
And animal contact, shock the refined,
But affected, sense with their stark naturalness.
Yet this is your prototype, who, season by season
Against siege of rain and the wind's attrition,
Preserves his stock, an impregnable fortress
Not to be stormed even in death's confusion.
Remember him, then, for he, too, is a winner of wars,
Enduring like a tree under the curious stars.

R.S. THOMAS (b.1913)

Pangur

Pangur, my cat (look) jumps,
Foreign to me, at the invisible
Mouse. He is back in my house
Where I am kept from by trying
To speak to you. And why have I
Been put into this ridiculous
Dream because I only wanted
To speak for once thoroughly
To another? Bring in the sea again.

I am not allowed the privilege
Of having Pangur here. At least
The mouse invisible I see.
I could entice it onto my knee
And let it speak for both of us.

W.S. GRAHAM (1918–86)

from The Aran Islands

This year Michael is busy in the daytime,
but at present there is a harvest moon,
and we spend most of the evening wandering about the island, looking out over
the bay where the shadows of the clouds
throw strange patterns of gold and black.
As we were returning through the village
this evening a tumult of revelry broke out
from one of the smaller cottages, and
Michael said it was the young boys and
girls who have sport at this time of the
year. I would have liked to join them, but
feared to embarrass their amusement.
When we passed on again the groups of
scattered cottages on each side of the way
reminded me of places I have sometimes
passed when travelling at night in France
or Bavaria, places that seemed so
enshrined in the blue silence of night one
could not believe they would reawaken.

Afterwards we went up on the Dun, where Michael said he had never been before after nightfall, though he lives within a stone's-throw. The place gains unexpected grandeur in this light, standing out like a corona of prehistoric stone upon the summit of the island. We walked round the top of the wall for some time looking down on the faint yellow roofs, with the rocks glittering beyond them, and the silence of the bay. Though Michael is sensible of the beauty of the nature round him, he never speaks of it directly, and many of our evening walks are occupied with long Gaelic discourses about the movements of the stars and moon.

J.M. SYNGE (1871–1909)

TIMES
AND
SEASONS
THE LIGHT WEIGHT
OF AN HOUR

The rhythm of dark and light and of the changing seasons as the year turned through its circle was as close to the Celts as the air they breathed. They celebrated each phase with festivals, taking great pleasure in the natural world and in enjoying the fresh delights that each new month would bring, not in any separate sense as observers but with a perception of themselves as part of the cosmos and the right order of things.

'Good, tranquil' autumn is followed by winter 'season of ice', and then May 'perfect month … claiming warm respect'. Each season was universally welcomed.

Despite this regularity and unbroken rhythm, for the poet time has an elastic quality which stretches and contracts according to what is being felt or experienced. The paradox is that time is measured and yet fluid.

At Strata Florida

This afternoon on the edge of autumn
our laughter feathers the quiet air
over tombs of princes. We idle
in an old nave, lightly approach
old altars. Our eyes, our hands
know fragments only; from these
the Abbey climbs and arches into the past.
We look up and find
only our own late August sky.

Ystrad Fflûr, your shadows fall
benevolently still on your ancient lands
and on us too, who touch your stones
not without homage. Take our laughter
on your consenting altars,
and to the centuries borne up
by your broken pillars, add
the light weight of an hour
at the end of summer.

RUTH BIDGOOD (b. 1922)

I Have Tidings For You

I have tidings for you;
the stag bells,
winter snows,
summer has gone.

Wind high and cold,
the sun low,
short its course,
the sea running high.

Crimson the bracken,
it has lost its shape,
the wild goose has raised
its accustomed cry.

Cold has seized
the birds' wings,
season of ice,
these are my tidings.

IRISH (9th century)
translated by K.H. JACKSON

May and January

Welcome, graceful greenwood choir,
Summer's month of May, for longing is mine.
Strong knight of loving favour,
Green-chained master of the wild wood;
Friend of love and birds,
The lore of lovers and their kinsman;
Courier of nine-times-twenty rendezvous,
Favourer of honoured meeting.
And great it is, by Mary, that he,
May, perfect month, is coming,
With his mind set, claiming warm respect,
On the conquest of every green glen.

A stout shelter, dresser of highways,
He clothed every place with his green web.
When there comes after frost's war
The thick-leaved tent (meadow's strength) –
Green are (chirping is my religion)
The paths of May in April's place –
Then come on the highest point of oak
Songs of the birds' chicks;
And a cuckoo at each field's edge,
And a warbler, and a long, lively day;
And pale mist behind the wind
Shielding the centre of the valley;
And a gay, bright sky of afternoon
Will there be, and handsome woods and green gossamer;
And hosts of birds on the trees,
And fresh leaves on tree-twigs;
And remembered will be Morfudd my golden girl,
And the thrill of seven-times-nine lovings.

Not like the surly, dark month
That rebukes every one for loving;
That makes sad rain and a short day,
And wind to plunder woods;
And weakness, the fragileness of fear,
And a long cloak and hailstone-rain,
And provokes tidal flow and cold,
And in streams grey deluges,
And a full roar in rivers,
And makes day angry and wrathful,
And the sky heavy and widely cold
With its colour veiling the moon.
May there come to him, swift sort of promise,
Double-bane for his boorishness!

DAFYDD AP GWILYM (c.1320–80)
translated by R.M. LOOMIS

A Good Tranquil Season is Autumn

A good tranquil season is Autumn;
there is occupation then for everyone
throughout the very short days.
Dappled fawns from the side of the hinds,
the red stalks of the bracken shelter them;
stags run from knolls
at the belling of the deer-herd.
Sweet acorns in the high woods,
corn-stalks about cornfields
over the expanse of the brown earth.
Prickly thorn-bushes of the bramble
by the midst of the ruined court;
the hard ground is covered with heavy fruit.
Hazelnuts of good crop fall
from the huge old trees of mounds.

IRISH

translated by K.H. JACKSON

from The Six Bards

⬚

First Bard

Night is dull and dark,
The clouds rest on the hillls;
No star with twinkling beam,
No moon looks from the skies.
I hear the blast in the wood,
But distant and dull I hear it.
The stream of the valley murmurs,
Low is its murmur too.
From the tree at the grave of the dead,
The lonely screech-owl groans.
I see a dim form on the plain,
'Tis a ghost! it fades, it flies;
Some dead shall pass this way.
From the lowly hut of the hill
The distant dog is howling;
The stag lies by the mountain-well,
The hind is at his side;
She hears the wind in his horns,
She starts, but lies again.
The roe is in the cleft of the rock:
The heath-cock's head beneath his wing.
No beast, no bird is abroad,
But the owl, and the howling fox;
She on the leafless tree,
He on the cloudy hill.
Dark, panting, trembling, sad,
The traveller has lost his way;
Through shrubs, through thorns he goes,
Beside the gurgling rills;
He fears the rock and the pool,
He fears the ghost of the night.
The old tree groans to the blast;
The falling branch resounds.
The wind drives the clung thorn

⬚
———

Along the sighing grass;
He shaked amid the night.
Dark, dusty, howling, is night,
Cloudy, windy, and full of ghosts;
The dead are abroad; my friends
Receive me from the night.

Second Bard
The wind is up on the mountain;
The shower of the hill descends.
Woods groan, and windows clap;
The growing river roars;
The traveller attempts the ford,
He falls, he shrieks, he dies.
The storm drives the horse from the hill,
The goat and the lowing cow;
They tremble as drives the shower,
And look for a shade of the stall.
The hunter starts from sleep in his lone hut,
And wakes the fire decay'd;
His wet dogs smoke around him:
He stops the chinks with heath.

Loud roar two mountain streams,
Which meet beside his booth.
Sad on the side of the hill
The wandering shepherd sits.
The tree resounds above him.
The stream roars down the rock.
He waits the rising moon
To lead him to his home.
Ghosts ride on the storm to-night.
Sweet is their voice between the gusts of wind,
Their songs are of other worlds.
   The rain is past. The dry winds blow.
Streams roar and windows clap;
Cold drops fall from the roof.
I see the starry sky. –
But the shower gathers again.
Dark, dark is the western sky!
Night is stormy, dismal, dark;
Receive me, my friends, from the night.

SCOTTISH

translated by JAMES MACPHERSON

from A Child's Christmas in Wales

Years and years and years ago,
when I was a boy, when there
were wolves in Wales, and birds
the colour of red-flannel
petticoats whisked past the harp-
shaped hills, when we sang and
wallowed all night and day in
caves that smelt like Sunday
afternoons in damp front
farmhouse parlours and we
chased, with the jawbones of
deacons, the English and the
bears, before the motor-car,
before the wheel, before the
duchess-faced horse, when we
rode the daft and happy hills
bareback, it snowed and it
snowed. But here a small boy
says: 'It snowed last year, too.
I made a snowman and my
brother knocked it down and I
knocked my brother down and
then we had tea.'

DYLAN THOMAS (1914–53)

LOVE
FAIREST OF THEM ALL

ove between a man and a woman has inspired some of the most moving and rapturous Celtic verse, but there is also a tenderness and delicacy to be found which is hard to equal. The loved one was extolled with an exuberant fervour often tempered with a sense of longing and hint of desolation. Dafydd ap Gwilym writes 'Unless I have the tenderest greeting, the girl will be my death.'

Unequalled intensity and passion are expressed by Celtic lovers who would travel through an 'acre of fire' and to whom love is worth more than 'an oven full of gold and silver'. However, despair and pain are never far away, for heartbreak and jealousy are close companions of love. The poet is tortured by memory and sits up all night with nothing to console him, 'growing thin on her account' and 'full of tears'.

I Know Where I'm Going

I know where I'm going
And I know who's going with me
I know who I love
And the Dear knows who I'll marry.

I'll give up silk stockings
And shoes of bright green leather
Combs to buckle my hair
And rings for every finger.

Feather beds are soft
And painted rooms are bonny
But I would trade them all
For my handsome, winsome Johnny.

Some say he's a bad one
But I say he's bonny
Fairest of them all
Is my handsome, winsome Johnny.

I know where I'm going
And I know who's going with me
I know who I love
And the Dear knows who I'll marry.

TRADITIONAL IRISH

The Blackthorn Pin

This blackthorn pin should not be in the
cloak on that white breast while there were
still, sweet red-lipped Mór, but one golden
brooch in Ireland.

It is not right to put in that cloak less than a
brooch of fine white bronze, or a marvellous
brooch of goldsmith's work, my sweet-
spoken red-lipped Mór.

Soft amber-coloured hair, steadfast graceful
girl who have deceived no man, it is not
fitting to put a blackthorn pin in your
chequered yellow cloak.

Peerless red cheek, nut of my heart, you
should not put in your yellow tartan cloak
but a brooch such as Gaibhneann might
have made.

Crimson cheek that I love, your green cloak
has seldom been without a gold brooch for a
single hour, but for this hour, O bright hand!

FEARCHAR O MAOILCHIARAIN (14th century)
translated by K.H. JACKSON

Love Song

In the white cabin at the foot of the mountain,
Is my sweet, my love:

Is my love, is my desire,
And all my happiness.

Before the night must I see her
Or my little heart will break.

My little heart will not break,
For my lovely dear I have seen.

Fifty nights I have been
At the threshold of her door; she did not know it.

The rain and the wind whipped me,
Until my garments dripped.

Nothing came to console me
Except the sound of breathing from her bed.

Except the sound of breathing from her bed,
Which came through the little hole of the key.

Three pairs of shoes I have worn out,
Her thought I do not know.

The fourth pair I have begun to wear,
Her thought I do not know.

Five pairs, alas, in good count,
Her thought I do not know.

– If it is my thought you wish to know,
It is not I who will make a mystery of it.

There are three roads on each side of my house,
Choose one among them.

Choose whichever you like among them,
Provided it will take you far from here.

– More is worth love, since it pleases me,
Than wealth with which I do not know what to do.

Wealth comes, and wealth it goes away,
Wealth serves for nothing.

Wealth passes like the yellow pears:
Love endures for ever.

More is worth a handful of love
Than an oven full of gold and silver.

BRETON (18th century)

translated by ALFRED M. WILLIAMS

Kellswater

Here's a health to you bonny Kellswater
Where you get all the pleasures of life
Where you get all the fishing and fowling
And a bonny wee lass for your wife.

Oh it's down where yon waters run muddy
I'm afraid they will never run clear
And it's when I begin for to study
My mind is on him that's not here.

And it's this one and that one may court him
But if any one gets him but me
It's early and late I will curse them
The parting lovely Willie from me.

Oh a father he calls on his daughter
Two choices I'll give unto thee
Would you rather see Willie's ship a'sailing
See him hung like a dog on yonder tree.

Oh father, dear father, I love him
I can no longer hide it from thee
Through an acre of fire I would travel
Along with the lovely Willie to be.

Oh hard was the heartbreak I'm finding
She took from her full heart's delight
May the chains of old Ireland come find them
And softly their pillows at night.

Oh yonder there's a ship on the ocean
And she does not know which way to steer
From the east and the west she's a'blowing
She reminds me of the charms of my dear.

Oh it's yonder my Willie will be coming
He said he'd be here in the spring
And it's down by yon green shades I'll meet him
And among wild roses we'll sing.

For a gold ring he placed on my finger
Saying love bear this in your mind
If ever I sail from old Ireland
You'll mind I'll not leave you behind.

Here's a health to you bonny Kellswater
Where you get all the pleasures of life
Where you get all the fishing and fowling
And a bonny wee lass for your wife.

TRADITONAL IRISH

The Seagull

Surely, fair gull on the tide,
Of the same colour as snow or the white moon,
Your beauty is unspotted,
A fragment like sun, gauntlet of the salt sea.
Light you are on the ocean wave,
Swift, proud, fish-eating bird.
There you'd go at anchor,
Hand in hand with me, sea lily.
Fashioned like writing paper shining in nature,
A nun atop the sea-tide are you.

With well-made praise for a girl, you shall have praise afar,
Seek the bend of a fort and castle.
Look, seagull, whether you may see
A girl of Eigr's colour on the fine fort.
Say my harmonious words.
Let her choose me, go to the girl.
She'd be by herself, dare to greet her.
Be adroit with the polished girl
For profit; say that I won't
(A refined, gentle lad) live unless I have her.

I love her, full assurance of joy,
Alas, men, never loved
Healthy Myrddin of flattery's lip
Or Taliesin a prettier girl!
The face of a sought-for girl under copper,
Supreme beauty very perfect and right.

Alas, gull, if you get to see
The cheek of the loveliest girl in Christendom,
Unless I have the tenderest greeting,
The girl will be my death.

DAFYDD AP GWILYM (c.1325–80)

translated by R.M. LOOMIS

The Lark in the Clear Air

Dear thoughts are in my mind
And my soul soars enchanted
As I hear the sweet lark sing
In the clear air of day.
For a tender beaming smile
To my hope has been granted
And tomorrow she shall hear
All my fond heart would say.

I shall tell her all my love
All my soul's adoration
And I think she will hear me
And will not say me nay.
It is this that gives my soul
All its joyous elation
As I hear the sweet lark sing
In the clear air of the day.

TRADITIONAL IRISH

She Moved Through the Fair

My young love said to me, 'My brothers won't mind,
And my parents won't slight you for your lack of kind.'
Then she stepped away from me, and this she did say,
'It will not be long, love, till our wedding day.'

She stepped away from me and she moved through the fair,
And fondly I watched her go here and go there,
Then she went her way homeward with one star awake,
As the swan in the evening moves over the lake.

The people were saying no two were e'er wed
But one had a sorrow that never was said,
And I smiled as she passed with her goods and her gear,
And that was the last that I saw of my dear.

I dreamt it last night that my young love came in,
So softly she entered, her feet made no din;
She came close beside me, and this she did say,
'It will not be long, love, till our wedding day.'

PADRAIC COLUM (1881–1972)

He Whose Hand and Eye Are Gentle

To tell you from the start, I have lost him whose hand and eye are gentle;
I shall go to seek him of the slender eyebrows, wherever the most
generous and fairest of men may be.

I shall go to the midst of Gwent without delaying, to the south I shall go
to search, and charge the sun and the moon to seek for him whose hand
and eye are gentle.

I shall search through all the lands, in the valley and on the mountain, in
the church and in the market, where is he whose hand and eye are gentle.

Mark you well, my friends, where you see a company of gentlemen,
who is the finest and most loving of them; that is he whose hand and eye
are gentle.

As I was walking under the vine the nightingale bade me rest, and it
would get information for me where was he whose hand and eye are
gentle.

The cuckoo said most kindly that she herself was quite well informed,
and would send her servant to inquire without ceasing where was he
whose hand and eye are gentle.

The cock-thrush advised me to have faith and hope, and said he himself
would take a message to him whose hand and eye are gentle.

The blackbird told me she would travel to Cambridge and to Oxford,
and would not complete her nest till she found him whose hand and eye
are gentle.

I know that he whose speech is pleasant can play the lute and play the
organ; God gave the gift of every music to him whose hand and eye are
gentle.

Hunting with hawks and hounds and horses, catching and calling and
letting slip, none loves a slim dog or a hound like him whose hand and
eye are gentle.

WELSH (16th century)

translated by K.H. JACKSON

My Love's an Arbutus

My love's an arbutus by the borders of Lene
So slender and shapely in her girdle of green
And I measure the pleasure of her eyes' sapphire sheen
By the blue skies that sparkle through that soft branching screen.

But though ruddy the berry and snowy the flower
That brighten together the arbutus bower
Perfuming and blooming through sunshine and shower
Give me her bright lips and her laugh's pearly dower.

TRADITIONAL IRISH

from Iona: Balva

Balva the old monk I am called: when I was
    young, Balva Honeymouth.
That was before Colum the White came to Iona
    in the West.
She whom I loved was a woman whom I won
    out of the South.
And I had a good heaven with my lips on hers
    and with breast to breast.

Balva the old monk I am called: were it not for
    the fear
That the soul of Colum the White would meet
    my soul in the Narrows
That sever the living and dead, I would rise up
    from here,
And go back to where men pray with spears
    and arrows.

Balva the old monk I am called: ugh! ugh! the
    cold bell of the matins – 'tis dawn!
Sure it's a dream I have had that I was in a
    warm wood with the sun ashine,
And that against me in the pleasant greenness
    was a soft fawn,
And a voice that whispered "Balva
    Honeymouth, drink, I am thy wine!"

FIONA MACLEOD (1855–1905)

from Líadaín and Cuirithir

'I am Líadaín,
I loved Cuirithir;
a truer word is never said.

A little while
I was with Cuirithir:
he liked my company.

Music of woods
sang to me by Cuirithir's side,
and the sound of the violent sea.

I wish
that Cuirithir would not be hurt
by any date I might arrange.

I cannot hide!
He was the treasure of my heart,
though I loved everyone besides.

A roar of flame
has burst my heart –
for certain, without him it cannot beat!'

And how she angered him
was, that she took the veil so quickly.

When he heard that she
was coming from the west,
he went on a currach
on the sea and took to
pilgrimage, so that she
never saw him again.
"He is gone now!" she said.

She remained on the stone
where he used to pray
until she died, and her soul
went to heaven. And
that stone was laid over
her face.

IRISH (9th century)
translated by KUNO MEYER

Down by the Salley Gardens

Down by the salley gardens my love and I did meet;
She passed the salley gardens with little snow-white feet.
She bid me take love easy, as the leaves grow on the tree;
But I, being young and foolish, with her would not agree.

In a field by the river my love and I did stand,
And on my leaning shoulder she laid her snow-white hand.
She bid me take life easy, as the grass grows on the weirs;
But I was young and foolish, and now am full of tears.

W.B. YEATS (1865–1939)

Mairi's Wedding

Step we gaily on we go
Heel for heel and toe for toe
Arm in arm and row in row
All for Mairi's wedding.

Over hillways up and down
Myrtle green and bracken brown
Past the shielings, thro' the town
All for sake o' Mairi.

Red her cheeks as rowans are
Bright her eye as any star
Fairest o' them a' by far
Is our darling Mairi.

Plenty herring, plenty meal
Plenty peat to fill her creel
Plenty bonnie bairns as weel
That's the toast for Mairi.

Step we gaily on we go
Heel for heel and toe for toe
Arm in arm and row in row
All for Mairi's wedding.

TRADITIONAL HEBRIDEAN

The Swallows

To our village a pathway small
Leadeth from the manor-hall;

A pathway whiter than 'tis wide,
And a May-bush grows beside:

Sweet thereon the May-flowers smell –
Our lord's young son, he loves them well.

I'd be a May-flower, an' I might,
For him to cull with his hand so white;

To cull with that small hand of his,
That whiter than the May-flower is.

I would a May-flower I might be,
That on his heart he might set me.

Still from the hall away he goes
When winter crowns the house with snows;

Goes to the country of the Gaul,
As doth the swallow, at winter-fall.

When the young year wakes germ and grain,
With the young year he comes again;

When the blue corn-flower's in the wheat,
And barley-ears wave green and sweet;

When sings the lark above the lea,
And finch and linnet on the tree; –

Comes back to us a welcome guest,
At holiday and patrons' feast.

Oh, would that every month were May,
And every hour a holiday:

Would I could see about the sky
All the year round the swallows fly;

Could see them still, from spring to spring,
Around our chimney on the wing!

BRETON (19th century)
translated by TOM TAYLOR

The Mist

Yesterday, Thursday, a day for drinking
(It was good for me to get), a gift came to me,
An omen of great import (I'm thin on her account),
A full love, I got
A session of sweet song under the greenwood
With a girl, she allows me a tryst.

There was not, under the joyful God the Father,
May a gift be hers, one man who knew,
When it was Thursday, at break of day,
How full of gladness I was,
Going (seeing her fine form)
To the land where the tall, slender sweetheart was,
When there came in truth on the long moor
A mist like night;
A great roll that was a surface to the rain,
Grey ranks to block me;
A tin sieve rusting,
The dark earth's bird net;
A dim hedge in a narrow path,
A slovenly blanket in the sky.
A grey cowl turning the ground the same colour,
A covert on every great, hollow valley.
High roofs to be seen,
A great bruise above the ridge, the land's exhalation.
Thick, grey, dunwhite, fragile fleece,
Same colour as smoke, the meadow's cowl,
A hedge of rain to block progress,
Armour of an oppressive host,
It would deceive men, dark of form,
Rude cloak of earth.
Towers of lofty state,
Of Gwyn's Family, a province of the wind.
Its dour cheeks hide the land,
Torches reaching to the zodiac.

Darkness, a thick, ugly one,
World's blindness to waylay a bard.
A wide web of costly cambric,
It was cast abroad like rope.
Spider's web, a French-shop product,
Headland-moor of Gwyn and his Family.
Brindled smoke that will abound,
The smoke of a circle of May-woods.
Unsightly fog where dogs bark,
Ointment of the hags of Annwn.
Clumsily like the dew it dampens,
Land's habergeon neither clear nor dry.

    It's easier to walk at night on the moors
On a journey than in mist by day;
The stars come out from the sky
Like flames of waxen candles;
But there does not come, dull, promised pain,
The moon or the Lord's stars in mist.
Rudely the mist made me bound with black
Ever, it was lightless;
Denied me a path under the sky,
Dark, grey veil that hinders love-messengers,
And kept me, a swift capture,
From going to my slim-browed woman.

DAFYDD AP GWILYM (c.1320–80)
translated by R.M. LOOMIS

SEA AND MINE

THE HEARTACHE
AND THE PAIN

Both fishing and mining have been part of the way of life for the Celtic peoples for thousands of years. This engagement with land and sea has engendered a deep respect for the elements. These are dangerous occupations and there is often a high price to pay for dependence on them as livelihoods. The harsh and sometimes brutal conditions experienced by fishermen of the 'wind, the wave, the tide' with only 'Sweet Christ the fisher' for comfort is matched by the grim reality of the miners' working conditions where 'all the air was black with sulphur and burning up the blood'. So we can appreciate the affecting simplicity of the Cornish fisherman's prayer for 'some fishes and a dry, safe bed'.

Fisherman's Prayer

At chapel, pier or out at sea
Sweet Christ the fisher comfort me.
Suffice for me my daily bread,
Some fishes and a dry, safe bed.

You know the heartache and the pain
Men's foolish hopes, the empty seine.
In modesty my prayers are said,
Some fishes and a dry, safe bed.

Temper the wind, the wave, the tide
Faith my lodestone, you my guide.
Blessed were the fishers so 'tis said,
Pray fishes and a dry, safe bed.

PRAYER BY WARWICK IN
ST LEONARD'S FISHERMEN'S CHAPEL,
ST IVES, CORNWALL

Breton Fisherman's Prayer

Protect me, O Lord, for my boat is so small,
Protect me, O Lord, for my boat is so small.
My boat is so small, and your sea is so wide.
Protect me, O Lord.

TRADITIONAL BRETON

from The Mine

A mine spread out its vast machinery.
Here engines, with their huts and smoky stacks,
Cranks, wheels, and rods, boilers and hissing steam,
Press'd up the water from the depths below.
Here fire-whims ran till almost out of breath,
And chains cried sharply, strain'd with fiery force.
Here blacksmiths hammer'd by the sooty forge,
And there a crusher crash'd the copper ore.
Here girls were cobbing under roofs of straw,
And there were giggers at the oaken hutch.
Here a man-engine glided up and down,
A blessing and a boon to mining men:
And near the spot where, many years before,
Turn'd round and round the rude old water wheel,
A huge fire-stamps was working evermore,
And slimy boys were swarming at the trunks.
The noisy lander by the trap-door bawl'd
With pincers in his hand; and troops of maids
With heavy hammers brake the mineral stones.
The cart-man cried, and shook his broken whip;
And on the steps of the account-house stood
The active agent, with his eye on all.

Below were caverns grim with greedy gloom,
And levels drunk with darkness; chambers huge
Where Fear sat silent, and the mineral-sprite
For ever chanted his bewitching song;
Shafts deep and dreadful, looking darkest things
And seeming almost running down to doom;
Rock under foot, rock standing on each side;
Rock cold and gloomy, frowning overhead;
Before, behind, at every angle, rock.
Here blazed a vein of precious copper ore,
Where lean men labour'd with a zeal for fame,
With face and hands and vesture black as night,
And down their sides the perspiration ran

In steaming eddies, sickening to behold.
But they complain'd not, digging day and night,
And morn and eve, with lays upon their lips.
Here yawn'd a tin-cell like a cliff of crags,
And Danger lurk'd among the groaning rocks,
And ofttimes moan'd in darkness. All the air
Was black with sulphur burning up the blood.
A nameless mystery seem'd to fill the void,
And wings all pitchy flapp'd among the flints,
And eyes that saw not sparkled mid the spars.
Yet here men work'd, on stages hung in ropes,
With drills and hammers blasting the rude earth,
Which fell with such a crash that he who heard
Cried, "Jesu, save the miner!" Here were ends
Cut through hard marble by the miners' skill,
And winzes, stopes and rises: pitches here,
Where work'd the heroic, princely tributer,
This month for nothing, next for fifty pounds.
Here lodes ran wide, and there so very small
That scarce a pick-point could be press'd between;
Here making walls as smooth as polish'd steel,
And there as craggy as a rended hill.
And out of sparry vagues the water oozed,
Staining the rock with mineral, so that oft
It led the labourer to a house of gems.
Across the mine a hollow cross-course ran
From north to south, an omen of much good;
And tin lay heap'd on stulls and level-plots;
And in each nook a tallow taper flared,
Where pale men wasted with exhaustion huge.
Here holes exploded, and there mallets rang,
And rocks fell crashing, lifting the stiff hair
From time-worn brows, and noisy buckets roar'd
In echoing shafts; and through this gulf of gloom
A hollow murmur rush'd for evermore.

JOHN HARRIS (1820–84)

Description of a Pit in Pontypridd

In a few minutes we were descending in the cage.
The water from the sides of the shaft dripped
steadily on us, and soon we were at the bottom,
more than a thousand feet from the surface. We were
led along a passage to a central gallery, from which
branched out various galleries leading to all parts of
the mine. Soon a number of men passed us, and
about 6.15 a collier rose and started the hymn,
"Guide me, O Thou Great Jehovah." At once it was
caught up by a large number of voices, and the
music was simply awe-inspiring. Then another rose
and offered up prayer that God would bless them
and keep them all day, and that He would put pure
thoughts and good desires in their hearts, and help
them to do their day's work for His sake.

After that a Welsh hymn was sung... By this time
several hundred men had gathered in the various
galleries, and altogether...there were more than
three hundred colliers, out of nearly five hundred
employed in the pit, at the prayer-meeting. A lad
recited with exquisite effect the fifteenth chapter of
John, in Welsh, and the melody of his utterance
came like a musical ripple on the air. From out of a
gallery, like a voice from the unseen, came an
address on the power of God to keep and save;
which was followed by the hymn, "Come ye that
love the Lord"... One felt the joy of the Lord surging
through the hearts of the colliers.

A Church clergyman from Durham prayed in English, and cited the 139th Psalm... When he came to
the words...

'The darkness and the light are both alike to Thee' –
then the presence of God overshadowed us as a glo-

rious blessing, and though in the gloom, lit up only by the feeble lights of the Davy lamps, we could scarcely distinguish any features of man, we felt that we were in the hollow of God's hand and full of joy unspeakable....

It was an awe-inspiring sight to see the lamps gleaming out of the blackness of the galleries; to hear the echoes of the musical choruses of the Welsh hymns ringing through the pit. Promptly at seven the service ended, and the colliers wended their way down the tunnels into the darkness, singing with gladness praises unto God.

When we reached the top of the shaft, day was just coming in over the mountains, and we felt that a newer day had dawned in the darkness underground, whose light was the Lamb.

from THE BAPTIST TIMES (1905)

from The Kelp Makers

The village of Trawbaun, which lies on the coast oppo-
site the Aran Islands, is a good instance of a kelp-making
neighbourhood. We reached it through a narrow road,
now in the hands of the relief workers, where we hur-
ried past the usual melancholy line of old men breaking
stones and younger men carrying bags of earth and sods.
Soon afterwards the road fell away quickly towards the
sea, through a village of many cottages huddled together,
with bare walls of stone that had never been white-
washed, as often happens in places that are peculiarly
poor. Passing through these, we came out on three or
four acres of sandhill that brought us to a line of rocks
with a narrow sandy cove between them just filling with
the tide. All along the coast, a little above high-water
mark, we could see a number of tall, reddish stacks of
dried seaweed, some of which had probably been standing for weeks, while others were in various unfinished
stages, or had only just been begun. A number of men
and women and boys were hard at work in every direction, gathering fresh weed and spreading it out to dry on
the rocks. In some places the weed is mostly gathered
from the foreshore; but in this neighbourhood, at least in
the early summer, it is pulled up from rocks under the
sea at low water, by men working from a boat or curagh
with a long pole furnished with a short crossbar nailed
to the top, which they entangle in the weeds. Just as we
came down, a curagh, lightly loaded by two boys, was
coming in over a low bar into the cove I have spoken of,
and both of them were slipping over the side every
moment or two to push their canoe from behind. Several
bare-legged girls, crooning merry songs in Gaelic, were
passing backwards and forwards over the sand, carrying

heavy loads of weed on their backs. Further out many other curaghs, more heavily laden, were coming slowly in, waiting for the tide; and some old men on the shore were calling out directions to their crews in the high-pitched tone that is so remarkable in this Connaught Irish. The whole scene, with the fresh smell of the sea and the blueness of the shallow waves, made a curious contrast with the dismal spectacle of the relief workers we had just passed, for here the people seemed as light-hearted as a party of schoolboys.

J.M. SYNGE (1871–1909)

Mingulay Boat Song

Hill you ho, boys
Let her go, boys
Bring her head round, now all together.
Hill you ho, boys
Let her go, boys
Sailing home, home to Mingulay.

What care we though white the Minch is?
What care we for wind or weather?
Let her go boys! every inch is
Wearing home, home to Mingulay.

Wives are waiting on the bank, or
Looking seaward from the heather.
Pull her round boys! and we'll anchor
Ere the sun sets at Mingulay.

What care we for hail or sleet?
What care we for wind or weather?
Pull her round, boys! every inch is
Wearing home, home to Mingulay.

TRADITIONAL SCOTTISH

The Rhondda

Hum of shaft-wheel, whirr and clamour
Of steel hammers overbeat, din down
Water-hag's slander. Greasy Rhondda
River throws about the boulders
Veils of scum to mark the ancient
Degraded union of stone and water.

Unwashed colliers by the river
Gamble for luck the pavements hide.
Kids float tins down dirty rapids.
Coal-dust rings the scruffy willows.
Circe is a drab.
She gives men what they know.
Daily to her pitch-black shaft
Her whirring wheels suck husbands out of sleep.
She for her profit takes their hands and eyes.

But the fat flabby-breasted wives
Have grown accustomed to her ways.
They scrub, make tea, peel the potatoes
Without counting the days.

ALUN LEWIS (1915–44)

PATRIOTISM
LAND OF MY FATHERS

Celts are different. They have a unique history, family of languages and cultural inheritance. Thus the poet describes how his nation lay like a lion 'bleeding in fetters' with 'green robe so faded' because for much of the last thousand years this separate identity has been submerged; but more recently a sense of nationhood has resurfaced in the Celtic lands. Patriotism, described as 'lightning in my blood', has produced many stirring poems and hymns to quicken the heart and imagination. Sometimes this desire for national and cultural identity has generated feelings of frustration and hopelessness, at other times strong sentiments of pride and expectation. Ultimately it is the place, the land, that matters to the patriot: this is the 'land of my fathers' and even though it often 'breaks the heart', it is still 'our home'.

The Little White Rose
(To John Gawsworth)

The rose of all the world is not for me.
I want for my part
Only the little white rose of Scotland
That smells sharp and sweet – and breaks the heart.

HUGH MACDIARMID (1892–1978)

The Harp That Once Thro' Tara's Halls

The harp, that once thro' Tara's halls
　　The soul of music shed,
Now hangs as mute on Tara's walls
　　As if that soul were fled.
So sleeps the pride of former days,
　　So glory's thrill is o'er
And hearts, that once beat high for praise,
　　Now feel that pulse no more.

No more to chiefs and ladies bright
　　The harp of Tara swells;
The chord alone, that breaks at night,
　　Its tale of ruin tells.
Thus freedom now so seldom wakes,
　　The only throb she gives
Is when some heart indignant breaks,
　　To show that still she lives.

THOMAS MOORE (1779–1852)

Dark Rosaleen

O my dark Rosaleen,
    Do not sigh, do not weep!
The priests are on the ocean green,
    They march along the Deep.
There's wine…from the royal Pope
    Upon the ocean green;
And Spanish ale shall give you hope,
    My Dark Rosaleen!
    My own Rosaleen!
Shall glad your heart, shall give you hope,
Shall give you health, and help, and hope,
    My Dark Rosaleen.

Over hills and through dales,
    Have I roamed for your sake;
All yesterday I sailed with sails
    On river and on lake.
The Erne…at its highest flood,
    I dashed across unseen,
For there was lightning in my blood,
    My Dark Rosaleen!
    My own Rosaleen!
Oh! there was lightning in my blood,
Red lightning lightened through my blood,
    My Dark Rosaleen!

All day long in unrest
    To and fro do I move,
The very soul within my breast
    Is wasted for you, love!
The heart…in my bosom faints
    To think of you, my Queen,
My life of life, my saint of saints,
    My Dark Rosaleen!
    My own Rosaleen!

To hear your sweet and sad complaints,
My life, my love, my saint of saints,
    My Dark Rosaleen!

Woe and pain, pain and woe,
    Are my lot night and noon,
To see your bright face clouded so,
    Like to the mournful moon.
But yet...will I rear your throne
    Again in golden sheen;
'Tis you shall reign, shall reign alone,
    My Dark Rosaleen!
    My own Rosaleen!
'Tis you shall have the golden throne,
'Tis you shall reign, and reign alone,
    My Dark Rosaleen!

Over dews, over sands
    Will I fly for your weal;
Your holy delicate white hands
    Shall girdle me with steel.
At home...in your emerald bowers,
    From morning's dawn till e'en,
You'll pray for me, my flower of flowers,
    My Dark Rosaleen!
    My own Rosaleen!
You'll think of me through daylight's hours,
My virgin flower, my flower of flowers,
    My Dark Rosaleen!

I could scale the blue air,
    I could plough the high hills,
Oh, I could kneel all night in prayer,
    To heal your many ills!
And one...beamy smile from you
    Would float like light between
My toils and me, my own, my true,
    My Dark Rosaleen!

My fond Rosaleen!
Would give me life and soul anew,
A second life, a soul anew,
   My Dark Rosaleen!

O! the Erne shall run red
   With redundance of blood,
The earth shall rock beneath our tread,
   And flames wrap hill and wood,
And gun-peal, and slogan cry,
   Wake many a glen serene,
Ere you shall fade, ere you shall die,
   My Dark Rosaleen!
   My own Rosaleen!
The Judgement Hour must first be nigh,
Ere you can fade, ere you can die,
   My Dark Rosaleen!

JAMES CLARENCE MANGAN (1803–49)

Skye Boat Song

Speed, bonnie boat, like a bird on the wing,
'Onward', the sailors cry;
Carry the lad that's born to be king
Over the sea to Skye.

Loud the winds howl, loud the waves roar,
Thunder clouds rend the air;
Baffled, our foes stand by the shore,
Follow they will not dare.

Though the waves leap, soft shall ye sleep,
Ocean's a royal bed.
Rocked in the deep, Flora will keep
Watch by your weary head.

Many's the lad fought on that day,
Well the claymore could wield,
When the night came, silently lay
Dead on Culloden's Field.

Burned are our homes, exile and death
Scatter the loyal men;
Yet ere the sword cool in the sheath,
Charlie will come again.

Speed, bonnie boat, like a bird on the wing,
'Onward', the sailors cry;
Carry the lad that's born to be king
Over the sea to Skye.

TRADITIONAL SCOTTISH

from Wild Wales

Next morning I set out to ascend Dinas Bran, a number of children, almost entirely girls, followed me. I asked them why they came after me. 'In the hope that you will give us something,' said one in very good English. I told them that I should give them nothing, but they still followed me. A little way up the hill I saw some men cutting hay. I made an observation to one of them respecting the fineness of the weather; he answered civilly, and rested on his scythe, whilst the others pursued their work. I asked him whether he was a farming man; he told me he was not; that he generally worked at the flannel manufactory, but that for some days past he had not been employed there, work being slack, and had on that account joined the mowers in order to earn a few shillings. I asked him how it was he knew how to handle a scythe, not being bred up a farming man; he smiled, and said that, somehow or other, he had learnt to do so.

'You speak very good English,' said I, 'have you much Welsh?'
'Plenty,' said he; 'I am a real Welshman.'
'Can you read Welsh?' said I.
'Oh, yes!' he replied.
'What books have you read?' said I.
'I have read the Bible, sir, and one or two other books.'
'Did you ever read the Bardd Cwsg?' said I.
He looked at me with some surprise. 'No,' said he, after a moment or two, 'I have never read it. I have seen it, but it was far too deep Welsh for me.'
'I have read it,' said I.
'Are you a Welshman?' said he.
'No,' said I; 'I am an Englishman.'
'And how is it,' said he, 'that you can read Welsh without being a Welshman?'

'I learned to do so,' said I, 'even as you learned to mow,
   without being bred up to farming work.'
'Ah!' said he, 'but it is easier to learn to mow than to read
   the Bardd Cwsg.'
'I don't know that,' said I; 'I have taken up a scythe a
   hundred times, but I cannot mow.'
'Will your honour take mine now, and try again?' said he.
'No,' said I, 'for if I take your scythe in hand I must give
   you a shilling, you know, by mowers' law.'

He gave a broad grin, and I proceeded up the hill. When
he rejoined his companions he said something to them in
Welsh, at which they all laughed. I reached the top of the
hill, the children still attending me.

GEORGE BORROW (1803–81)

Erin

I dreamt that a lion lay bleeding in fetters,
    Fast bound on an isle of the far Western wave,
And I saw on his front, scarred with fire-branded letters,
    "Behold the Earth's scorned one – *a satisfied slave.*"

O Erin, alas! is thy green robe so faded,
    Since tyrants have blasted thy beautiful plains?
Are thy sons – oh, how fallen! – so deeply degraded,
    As tamely to list to the clank of their chains?

Poor serf! canst thou slumber? I feel my blood burning,
    I sink – crimsoned o'er with the blushes of shame:
Arise! and the thrall of your fell despots spurning,
    Give the harp-blazoned banner to battle and fame.

Do the deep echoes mock me, or hear I a sound
    As of far-distant billows collecting their might,
While hollowly thunder-peals mutter around?
    Yes! Yes! Lo the nation's upspringing to fight!

At length the dread spirit of Liberty rallies:
    Hark! list how the crown-crushing avalanche roars!
Arouse ye to war from your thousand green valleys,
    Be strong as the ocean that lashes your shores.

Brave bondsmen, arise! shout aloud o'er the waters,
 "We swear by our altars, our sires, and their graves,
No longer, loved land, shall thy sorrowing daughters
 Be consorts and mothers of spiritless slaves."

In the shock of the conflict, our wild harp uprearing,
 Spill freely the best blood each bosom affords;
Heaven prosper the shamrock – wreathed ensign of Erin,
 And, God of the Patriot, breathe on our swords.

RICHARD D'ALTON WILLIAMS (1822–62)

The Song of the Western Men

A good sword and a trusty hand!
A merry heart and true!
King James's men shall understand
What Cornish lads can do!

And have they fixed the where and when?
And shall Trelawny die?
Here's twenty thousand Cornish men
Will know the reason why!

Out spake their Captain brave and bold:
A merry wight was he:–
"If London Tower were Michael's hold,
We'd set Trelawny free!

"We'll cross the Tamar, land to land:
The Severn is no stay:
With 'one and all,' and hand in hand;
And who shall bid us nay?

"And when we come to London Wall,
A pleasant sight to view,
Come forth! come forth! ye cowards all:
Here's men as good as you.

"Trelawny he's in keep and hold:
Trelawny he may die:
But here's twenty thousand Cornish bold
Will know the reason why!"

R.S. HAWKER (1803–75)

King Billy on the Walls

I can remember looking up at him
on many a Belfast wall; King Billy, bright
in his chalk colours, riding a white horse,
larger than life, twice as victorious.

If I saw him again, perhaps I'd see
the sick, frail Dutchman with the tired eyes
who looked down on the drums, the exuberance,
the orange sashes, with an embarrassed air,

wondering when he became so popular.
And now he looks on fear and scattered flesh
and brutal faces, thinking of the years he lost
fighting the French, the Irish, his wife's father…

He was a gentle man, and all his life
a soldier, and now, trapped in the crude chalk
both friends and enemies use to picture him,
his eyes can still rest nowhere but on pain.

SHEENAGH PUGH (b. 1950)

Bruce's March to Bannockburn

Scots, wha hae wi' Wallace bled,
Scots, wham Bruce has aften led,
Welcome to your gory bed,
    Or to Victorie!

Now's the day, and now's the hour;
See the front o' battle lour:
See approach proud Edward's power –
    Chains and slaverie!

Wha will be a traitor knave?
Wha can fill a coward's grave?
Wha sae base as be a slave?
    Let him turn and flee!

Wha, for Scotland's King and Law,
Freedom's sword will strongly draw,
Free-man stand, or Free-man fa',
    Let him on wi' me!

By oppression's woes and pains!
By your sons in servile chains!
We will drain our dearest veins,
    But they shall be free!

Lay the proud usurpers low!
Tyrants fall in every foe!
Liberty's in every blow!
    Let us do or die!

ROBERT BURNS (1759–96)

The Minstrel Boy

The Minstrel Boy to the war is gone,
In the ranks of death you'll find him;
His father's sword he has girded on,
And his wild harp slung behind him.
'Land of song!' said the warrior bard,
'Though all the world betrays thee
One sword, at least, thy rights shall guard,
One faithful harp shall praise thee.'

The minstrel fell – but the foeman's chain
Could not bring his proud soul under;
The harp he loved ne'er spoke again
For he tore its chords asunder;
And said, 'No chains shall sully thee,
Thou soul of love and bravery!
Thy songs were made for the brave and free,
They shall never sound in slavery!'

THOMAS MOORE (1779–1852)

Such a Parcel of Rogues in a Nation

Fareweel to a' our Scottish fame,
    Fareweel our ancient glory!
Fareweel ev'n to the Scottish name,
    Sae famed in martial story!
Now Sark rins o'er the Solway sands,
    An' Tweed rins to the ocean,
To mark where England's province stands –
    Such a parcel of rogues in a nation!

What force or guile could not subdue
    Thro' many warlike ages
Is wrought now by a coward few
    For hireling traitor's wages.
The English steel we could disdain,
    Secure in valour's station;
But English gold has been our bane –
    Such a parcel of rogues in a nation!

O, would, or I had seen the day
    That Treason thus could sell us,
My auld grey head had lien in clay
    Wi' Bruce and loyal Wallace!
But pith and power, till my last hour
    I'll mak this declaration: –
'We're bought and sold for English gold' –
    Such a parcel of rogues in a nation!

ROBERT BURNS (1759–96)

The Land of My Fathers

O land of my fathers, O land of my love,
Dear mother of minstrels who kindle and move,
And hero on hero, who at honour's proud call,
For freedom their life-blood let fall.
> Wales! Wales! O but my heart is with you!
> And long as the sea
> Your bulwark shall be,
> To Cymru my heart shall be true.

O land of the mountains, the bard's paradise,
Whose precipice proud, valleys lone as the skies,
Green murmuring forest, far echoing flood
Fire the fancy and quicken the blood.
> Wales! Wales! O but my heart is with you!
> And long as the sea
> Your bulwarks shall be,
> To Cymru my tongue shall be true!

For tho' the fierce foeman has ravaged your realm,
The old speech of Cymru he cannot o'erwhelm,
Our passionate poets to silence command
Or banish the harp from your strand.
> Wales! Wales! O but my heart is with you!
> And long as the sea
> Your bulwark shall be,
> To Cymru my heart shall be true!

EVAN JAMES (1846–1931)
translated by A.P. GRAVES

RELIGION
THE BLESSING
OF LIGHT

raise is at the heart of the Celtic Christian response to God, and it is a common and unifying experience. Indeed the whole of nature takes part in this hymn of glory as in the *Iona Benedicite* where all creation praises the Lord. Boundaries between the religious and the secular were difficult to define and for the Celt they didn't really exist: the worlds overlapped. Matter was pervaded by spirit, and the invisible world was as real and close as the visible and tangible. The ordinary things of life, the everyday tasks and familiar places become sacramental, and the poet finds that though he 'knew not the ways, Thy knowledge was around me'. Saints and angels were like friends who accompanied the believer on the pilgrim path and it was natural to invoke protection and to pray for help from them. While here on earth, to live closely to Christ and follow his example was the ideal, to be one who 'caught fire and burned steadily' until the soul finally left the body at death and went 'up, and off, and on its way to God'.

Iona

Iona of my love, Iona of my heart,
Instead of monks' voices
Shall be the lowing of cattle;
But ere the world shall come to an end
Iona shall be as it was.

attributed to SAINT COLUMBA (521–97)

An Irish Blessing

May the blessing of light be with you –
    light outside and light within.
May sunlight shine upon you and warm your heart
    'til it glows like a great peat fire
    so that the stranger may come and warm himself by it.
May a blessed light shine out of your two eyes
    like a candle set in two windows of a house,
    bidding the wanderer to come in out of the storm.
May you ever give a kindly greeting to those whom you pass
    as you go along the roads.
May the blessing of rain – the sweet, soft rain – fall upon you
    so that little flowers may spring up to shed their
    sweetness in the air.
May the blessings of the earth – the good, rich earth – be
    with you.
May the earth be soft under you when you rest upon it,
    tired at the end of the day.
May earth rest easy over you when at last you lie under it.
May earth rest so lightly over you that your spirit
    may be out from under it quickly,
    and up, and off,
    and on its way to God.

TRADITIONAL IRISH

from Carmina Gadelica

Thou great Lord of the sun,
  In the day of my need be near me;
Thou great Being of the universe,
  Keep me in the surety of Thine arms!

Leave me not in dumbness,
  Dead in the wilderness;
Leave me not to my stumbling,
  For my trust is in Thee, my Saviour!

Though I had no fire,
  Thy warmth did not fail me;
Though I had no clothing,
  Thy love did not forsake me.

Though I had no hearth,
  The cold did not numb me;
Though I knew not the ways,
  Thy knowledge was around me.

Though I was in weakness,
  The hinds showed me kindness;
Though I had no light,
  The night was as the day.

Though I had no bed,
  I lacked not for sleep,
For Christ's arm was my pillow,
  His eye supreme was my protection.

Though I was forlorn,
  Hunger came not near me,
For Christ's Body was my food,
  The Blood of Christ, it was my drink.

Though I was without reason,
    Thou forsookest me not a moment;
Though I was without sense,
    Thou didst not choose to leave me.

Though the stones were diamonds,
    Though they were dollars of gold,
Though the whole ocean were wine,
    Offered to me of right;

Though the earth were of cinnamon
    And the lakes were of honey,
Dearer were a vision of Christ
    In peace, in love, in pity.

Jesu, meet Thou my soul!
    Jesu, clothe me in Thy love!
Jesu, shield Thou my spirit!
    Jesu, stretch out to me Thine hand!

SCOTTISH

translated by ALEXANDER CARMICHAEL

The Chapel

A little aside from the main road,
becalmed in a last-century greyness,
there is the chapel, ugly, without the appeal
to the tourist to stop his car
and visit it. The traffic goes by,
and the river goes by, and quick shadows
of clouds, too, and the chapel settles
a little deeper into the grass.

But here once on an evening like this,
in the darkness that was about
his hearers, a preacher caught fire
and burned steadily before them
with a strange light, so that they saw
the splendour of the barren mountains
about them and sang their amens
fiercely, narrow but saved
in a way that men are not now.

R.S. THOMAS (b. 1913)

from The Life of Ciaran of Saighir

When Saint Ciaran came thither he sat down there straightway under a tree, beneath whose shade there was a most ferocious boar. The boar, seeing a man, at first fled in terror, but afterwards, becoming calmed by God, it returned as a servant to the man of God; and that boar was the first pupil as it were a monk to St Ciaran in that place. For of its own accord the boar straightway energetically cut with its tusks saplings and straw for material to construct a cell; for there was no one with God's saint at that time, since he had gone off from his pupils alone to that desert place. Thereupon other animals came to St Ciaran from the lairs of the wilderness, namely a fox and a badger and a deer, and remained with him in the greatest docility, for they obeyed the orders of the holy man in everything like monks. One day the Fox, who was more cunning and more wily than the other animals, stole the shoes of his abbot, namely St Ciaran, and abandoning his chosen path, took them to his old den in the wilderness, intending to devour them there. Learning this, the holy father Ciaran sent another monk or pupil, namely the Badger, to the wilderness after the Fox to bring back the brother to his place. And the Badger, who was well acquainted with the woods, obeying at once the word of his superior, set out and came straight to the cave of brother Fox; and when he found him about to devour the shoes of his master, he cut off his ears and tail and plucked out his hairs and compelled him to come with him to the monastery to do penance for his theft. And the Fox, compelled perforce, came along with the Badger to St Ciaran in his cell at nones, bringing the shoes unharmed. And the holy man said to the Fox, "Why have you done this sin, brother, which monks ought not to do? Behold, our water is pure and common to all, and the food likewise is apportioned to all in common; and if you had desired to eat flesh according to your instinct, almighty God would have made it for us from the bark of trees." Then the Fox, begging for forgiveness, did penance by fasting, and did not touch food until the holy man commanded it. Thereupon he remained in the fellowship of the others.

IRISH (9th–10th century)

translated by K.H. JACKSON

115

An Iona Benedicite

O ye angels of the Lord, bless ye the Lord,
    praise Him and magnify Him for ever.
O ye Saints of the Isles, bless ye the Lord.
O ye Servants of Christ who here sang God's
  praises and hence went forth to preach,
    bless ye the Lord.
O ye souls of the faithful, who rest in Jesus,
O ye kindly folk of the Island,
O ye pilgrims who seek joy and health in this
  beloved Isle,
    bless ye the Lord.
O ye sheep and hornèd cattle,
O ye lambs that gambol on the sward,
O ye seals that glisten in the waters,
    bless ye the Lord.
O ye ravens and hoodies,
O ye rooks that caw from the sycamores,
O ye buzzards that float on the wind-currents,
    bless ye the Lord.
O ye gulls that fill the beaches with your clamour,
O ye terns and gannets that dive headlong for
  your prey,
O ye curlews and landrails,
O ye pied shelduck and Bride's ghillies,
O ye dunlins that wheel in unison over the waves,
    bless ye the Lord.
O ye larks that carol in the heavens,
O ye blackbirds that pipe at the dawning,
O ye pipits and wheatears,
O ye warblers and wrens that make the glens
  joyful with song,
O ye bees that love the heather,
    bless ye the Lord.

O ye primroses and bluebells,
O ye flowerets that gem the marsh with colour,
O ye golden flags that deck Columba's Bay
with glory,
bless ye the Lord.
O ye piled rocks fashioned by Nature's might
thro' myriad ages,
O ye majestic Bens of Mull,
O ye white sands and emerald shallows,
O ye blue and purple deeps of ocean,
O ye winds and clouds, bless ye the Lord.
O all ye works of the Lord, bless ye the Lord,
praise Him and magnify Him for ever.

E.D. SEDDING, SSJE (b. 1884–d. 1973)

Saint Patrick's Breastplate

I bind unto myself today
The strong name of the Trinity:
By invocation of the same,
The Three in One and One in Three.

I bind this day to me for ever,
By power of faith, Christ's incarnation,
His baptism in the Jordan River,
His death on the Cross for my salvation.
His bursting from the spiced tomb,
His riding up the heavenly way,
His coming at the day of doom
I bind unto myself today!

I bind unto myself today
The power of God to hold and lead:
His eye to watch, his might to stay,
His ear to hearken to my need;
The wisdom of my God to teach,
His hand to guide, his shield to ward;
The Word of God to give me speech,
His heavenly host to be my guard!

Christ be with me, Christ within me,
Christ behind me, Christ before me,
Christ beside me, Christ to win me,
Christ to comfort and restore me.
Christ beneath me, Christ above me,
Christ in quiet, Christ in danger,
Christ in hearts of all that love me,
Christ in mouth of friend and stranger.

I bind unto myself the name,
The strong name of the Trinity:
By invocation of the same,
The Three in One and One in Three;
Of whom all nature hath creation,
Eternal Father, Spirit, Word;
Praise to the Lord of my salvation –
Salvation is of Christ the Lord!

IRISH

translated by C.F. ALEXANDER

St Kevin and the Blackbird

And then there was St Kevin and the blackbird.
The saint is kneeling, arms stretched out, inside
His cell, but the cell is narrow, so

One turned-up palm is out the window, stiff
As a crossbeam, when a blackbird lands
And lays in it and settles down to nest.

Kevin feels the warm eggs, the small breast, the tucked
Neat head and claws and, finding himself linked
Into the network of eternal life,

Is moved to pity: now he must hold his hand
Like a branch out in the sun and rain for weeks
Until the young are hatched and fledged and flown.

*

And since the whole thing's imagined anyhow,
Imagine being Kevin. Which is he?
Self-forgetful or in agony all the time

From the neck on out down through his hurting fore-arms?
Are his fingers sleeping? Does he still feel his knees?
Or has the shut-eyed blank of underearth

Crept up through him? Is there distance in his head?
Alone and mirrored clear in love's deep river,
'To labour and not to seek reward,' he prays,

A prayer his body makes entirely
For he has forgotten self, forgotten bird
And on the riverbank forgotten the river's name.

SEAMUS HEANEY (b. 1939)

Sans Day Carol

Now the holly bears a berry as white as the milk,
And Mary bore Jesus, Who was wrapped up in silk:

    And Mary bore Jesus Christ Our Saviour for to be,
    And the first tree in the greenwood, it was the
    holly, holly! holly!
    And the first tree in the greenwood, it was the holly.

Now the holly bears a berry as green as the grass,
And Mary bore Jesus, Who died on the Cross:

Now the holly bears a berry, as blood it is red,
Then trust we our Saviour, Who rose from the dead:

Now the holly bears a berry as black as the coal,
And Mary bore Jesus, Who died for us all:

    And Mary bore Jesus Christ Our Saviour for to be,
    And the first tree in the greenwood, it was the
    holly, holly! holly!
    And the first tree in the greenwood, it was the holly.

TRADITIONAL CORNISH

The Rune of St Patrick

At Tara to-day in this fateful hour
I place all Heaven with its power,
And the sun with its brightness,
And the snow with its whiteness,
And fire with all the strength it hath,
And lightning with its rapid wrath,
And the winds with their swiftness along their path,
And the sea with its deepness,
And the rocks with their steepness,
And the earth with its starkness:
    All these I place,
    By God's almighty help and grace,
Between myself and the powers of darkness.

IRISH

translated by CHARLES MANGAN

An Irish Blessing

May the road rise to meet you.
May the wind be always at your back.
May the sun shine warm upon your face,
   the rains fall soft
   upon your fields and,
   until we meet again,
May God hold you in the palm of his hand.

TRADITIONAL IRISH

WISDOM
THERE ARE
THREE THINGS

L ike all societies, the Celts have their own store of wisdom, a collection of proverbs and sayings built up over many generations. One must remember that the Celtic tribes inhabited and ruled much of northern Europe for hundreds of years before the Roman conquest of Gaul in the first century BC. There is, therefore, a continuity of tradition expressed in the passages recorded here. Originally these wise sayings would have been transmitted orally and they were grouped in threes to make them easier to remember. They contain a great deal of common sense and insight, not without a touch of humour here and there: 'usual for a portly person to be pompous'. Not only do they give us an understanding of the structure of Celtic society, but they give expression to a dialectic which embodied the relationship between these values and daily living.

from Druidic Triads: The Wisdom of the Cymry

※

Of Virtues

There are three things excellent among worldly
affairs: hating folly, loving virtue, and
endeavouring constantly to learn.

Three beautiful beings of the world: the godly,
the skilful, and the temperate.

Three tendencies of man's lifetime: hope, love,
and joy.

Three things excellent for a man: valour,
learning, and discretion.

Three things must be united before good can
come of them: thinking well, speaking well,
and acting well.

Three things are becoming for a man:
knowledge, good deeds, and gentleness.

Three things which strengthen a man to stand
against the whole world: seeing the quality and
beauty of truth, seeing beneath the cloak of
falsehood, and seeing to what ends truth and
falsehood come.

Three things it is everyone's duty to do: listen
humbly, answer discreetly, and judge kindly.

Three things a man should keep always before
him: his wordly duty, his conscience, and the
laws of God.

※

Three sureties of happiness for a man: good
habits, amiability, and forbearance.

Three manifestations of humanity: affectionate
bounty, a loving manner, and praiseworthy
knowledge.

Three things without which there can be
nothing good: truth, peace, and generosity.

Three godly deeds in a man: to forgive the
wrong done him, to amend everything he can,
and to refrain from injustice.

Three joys of the happy: abstinence, peace, and
constancy.

Three antagonists of goodness: pride, passion,
and covetousness.

Three things which spring from following
lawful goodness: universal love from the wise,
wordly sufficiency, and reward from God in the
life to come.

Three things beside which evil cannot be:
conformity to law, knowledge, and love.

Three things must wait long before they are
attained: honesty from covetousness, wisdom
from pride, and wealth from sloth.

Three things hard to obtain: cold fire, dry
water, and lawful covetousness.

Of the Upright Man

There are three kingdoms of the happy man:
the world's good word, a cheerful conscience,
and firm hope of the world to come.

Three leaderships of the happy man: being
good in his service, good in his disposition,
and good in his secrecy; and these are found
united only in the devout or the nobly born.

In three things a man is like God: justice,
knowledge, and mercy.

Three things lovable in a man: peace, wisdom,
and kindness.

Three chief virtues of a man: diligence,
sincerity, and humility.

Three things which show the true man: a silent
mouth, an incurious eye, and a fearless face.

Three companions on the high road to heaven:
a patient poor man, a reflective wise man, and a
tolerant reformer.

Three men who are loved by God: the strong
just man, the brave merciful man, and the man
generous without regret.

Three things without which immunity from
God cannot be: forgiving an enemy and a
transgression; generosity of judgment and act;
and cleaving to what is just, come what may
come.

There are three things to be commended in a man: wisdom in his talk, justice in his actions, and excess in nothing.

Of the Rewards of Virtue
There are three things which the happy will gain: prosperity, honour, and ease of conscience.

Three things which the humble will gain: plenty, joy, and the love of their neighbours.

Three things which the sincere will gain: favour, respect, and prosperity.

Three things which the patient will gain: love, peace, and succour.

Three things which the merciful will gain: favour, love, and God's mercy.

Three things which the godly will gain: worldly sufficiency, peace of conscience, and heavenly joy.

Three things which the industrious will gain: precedence, wealth, and praise from the wise.

Three things which the law-abiding will gain:
health, success, and honour.
Three things which the careful man will gain:
respect, plenty, and content.

Three things which the generous of heart will
gain: joy from his profit, felicity in giving, and
infinite profit in the end.

Three things which the early riser will gain:
health, wealth, and holiness.

WELSH

Usual is Wind From The South

Usual is wind from the south; usual a deposit
   in a church;
usual for a weak man to be thin;
usual for a person to ask for news;
usual for a foster-child to have luxuries.

Usual is wind from the east; usual for a portly
   person to be pompous;
usual a blackbird among thorns;
usual after great violence is great lamentation;
usual for ravens to get flesh in a wood.

Usual is wind from the north; usual for maids
   to be sweet;
usual is a handsome man in Gwynedd;
usual for a prince to provide a feast;
usual is despondency after drinking.

Usual is wind from the sea; usual the surge of
   flood-tide;
usual for a pig to breed swine-lice;
usual for swine to root up earth-nuts.

Usual is wind from the mountain; usual is
   a dullard in the country;
usual to get thatching in marshes;
usual for a cleric to be reared on milk;
usual are leaves and saplings and trees.

Usual from bastardy for men to be base
and for bad women to be feasted on mead,
and distress to be on the grandson, and the
   great-grandson to be worse and worse.

WELSH (*c.* 12th century)
translated by K.H. JACKSON

WARFARE

I SEE A BATTLE

In Celtic tribal society battles and skirmishes were an ever-present fact of life. Not only did the tribes fight against each other but they later resisted successive waves of invaders: Romans, Anglo-Saxons, Vikings and Normans. The war hero with his brow 'full of victories' held a special place among the people, and epic poems were often composed in honour of his achievements and martial conquests. These fearsome men and women were larger than life and the descriptions of their combat are often full of horror and gory bloodshed. Mourning was very deep if they were killed. Even though there was great honour in a glorious death in battle, sorrow was also expressed at the tragic demise and loss of a courageous leader. In defeat the Celts were often feared and admired for their bravery and fierce tempers – qualities which are still much in evidence today.

from The Táin (The Cattle Raid)

The Táin Bó Cuailnge Begins

...they saw a young grown girl in front of them. She had
yellow hair. She wore a speckled cloak fastened around her
with a gold pin, a red-embroidered hooded tunic and sandals
with gold clasps. Her brow was broad, her jaw narrow, her
two eyebrows pitch black, with delicate dark lashes casting
shadows half way down her cheeks. You would think her lips
were inset with Parthian scarlet. Her teeth were like an array
of jewels between the lips. She had hair in three tresses: two
wound upward on her head and a third hanging down her
back, brushing her calves. She held a light gold weaving-rod
in her hand, with gold inlay. Her eyes had triple irises. Two
black horses drew her chariot, and she was armed.

'What is your name?' Medb said to the girl.

'I am Fedelm, and I am a woman poet of Connacht.'

'Where have you come from?' Medb said.

'From learning verse and vision in Alba,' the girl said.

'Have you the *imbas forasnai*, the Light of Foresight?'
    Medb said.

'Yes I have,' the girl said.

'Then look for me and see what will become of my army.'
So the girl looked.

Medb said, 'Fedelm, prophetess; how seest thou the host?'
Fedelm said in reply:

'I see it crimson, I see it red.'

> 'I see a battle: a blond man
> with much blood about his belt
> and a hero-halo round his head.
> His brow is full of victories.
>
> Seven hard heroic jewels
> are set in the iris of his eye.
> His jaws are settled in a snarl.
> He wears a looped, red tunic.

A noble countenance I see,
working effect on womenfolk;
a young man of sweet colouring;
a form dragonish in the fray.

His great valour brings to mind
Cúchulainn of Murtheimne,
the hound of Culann, full of fame.
Who he is I cannot tell
but I see, now, the whole host
coloured crimson by his hand.

A giant on the plain I see,
doing battle with the host,
holding in each of his two hands
four short quick swords.

I see him hurling against that host
two *gae bolga* and a spear
and an ivory-hilted sword,
each weapon to its separate task.

He towers on the battlefield
in breastplate and red cloak.
Across the sinister chariot-wheel
the Warped Man deals death
– that fair form I first beheld
melted to a mis-shape.

I see him moving to the fray:
take warning, watch him well,
Cúchulainn, Sualdam's son!
Now I see him in pursuit.

Whole hosts he will destroy,
making dense massacre.
In thousands you will yield your heads.
I am Fedelm. I hide nothing.

The blood starts from warrior's wounds
– total ruin – at his touch:
your warriors dead, the warriors
of Deda mac Sin prowling loose;
torn corpses, women wailing,
because of him – the Forge-Hound.'

***

Single Combat
Cúchulainn made this chant:

'I am alone against hordes.
I can neither halt nor let pass.
I watch through the long hours
alone against all men.

Tell Conchobor to come now.
It wouldn't be too soon.
Mágach's sons have stolen our cattle
to divide between them.

I have held them single-handed,
but one stick won't make fire.
Give me two or three
and torches will blaze!

I am almost worn out
by single contests.
I can't kill all their best
alone as I am.'

***

Combat of Ferdia and Cúchulainn
The charioteer got up and brought the horses and yoked the
chariot. Cúchulainn got into the chariot and they pressed on
toward the ford. Ferdia's charioteer wasn't watching long

when he heard the creaking of the chariot as it drew near.
He woke his master and made this chant:

> 'I hear a chariot creaking.
> I see its yoke of silver
> and the great trunk of a man
> >   above the hard prow.
> The shafts jut forward,
> they are approaching us
> by the place of the tree-stump,
> >   triumphant and proud.
>
> There's a skilled Hound at the helm,
> a fine chariot-warrior,
> a wild hawk hurrying
> >   his horses southward.
> Surely it is Cúchulainn's
> chariot-horses coming.
> Who says he is not
> >   coming to our defeat?
>
> I had a dream last year:
> whoever, at the time appointed,
> opposes the Hound on the slope,
> >   let him beware.
> The Hound of Emain Macha,
> in all his different shapes,
> the Hound of plunder and battle
> >   – I hear him, and he hears.'

***

The charioteers sent the *gae bolga* down the stream. 'Beware
the *gae bolga*,' he said.

Cúchulainn caught it in the fork of his foot and sent it
casting toward Ferdia and it went through the deep and
sturdy apron of twice-smelted iron, and shattered in three
parts the stout strong stone the size of a mill-stone, and went

coursing through the highways and byways of his body so that every single joint filled with barbs.

'That is enough now,' Ferdia said, 'I'll die of that. There is strength in the thrust of your right foot. It is wrong I should fall at your hand.'

He said:

> 'Hound of the bright deeds,
> you have killed me unfairly.
> Your guilt clings to me
> as my blood sticks to you.
>
> By the way of deceit
> no good can come.
> I am struck dumb.
> I am leaving this life.
>
> My ribs are crushed in,
> my heart is all blood.
> I have not fought well.
> Hound, I am fallen.'

* * *

Cúchulainn stayed staring there at Ferdia.

'Well, friend Laeg,' Cúchulainn said, 'strip Ferdia now. Take off his gear and garments. Let me see the brooch he fought this furious battle for.'

Laeg came and stripped Ferdia and took off his gear and garments, and showed him the brooch. Cúchulainn mourned and lamented:

> 'Ferdia of the hosts
> and the hard blows, beloved
> golden brooch, I mourn
> your conquering arm
>
> and our fostering together,
> a sight to please a prince;
> your gold-rimmed shield,
> your slender sword,

138

the ring of bright silver
on your fine hand,
your skill at chess,
your flushed, sweet cheek,

your curled yellow hair
like a great lovely jewel,
the soft leaf-shaped belt
that you wore at your waist.

You have fallen to the Hound,
I cry for it, little calf.
The shield didn't save you
that you brought to the fray.

Shameful was our struggle,
the uproar and grief!
O fair, fine hero
who shattered armies
and crushed them under foot,
golden brooch, I mourn.'

'Now, friend Laeg,' Cúchulainn said, 'cut Ferdia open and
take the *gae bolga* out of him. I must have my weapon.'

IRISH (8th century)

translated by THOMAS KINSELLA

Connal

Autumn is dark on the mountains; grey mist rests on the hills. The whirlwind is heard on the heath. Dark rolls the river thro' the narrow plain. A tree stands alone on the hill, and marks the grave of Connal. The leaves whirl round with the wind, and strew the grave of the dead. At times are seen here the ghosts of the deceased, when the musing hunter alone stalks slowly over the heath. Appear in thy armour of light, thou ghost of mighty Connal! Shine, near thy tomb, Crimora! like a moon-beam from a cloud.

Who can search the source of thy race, O Connal? and who recount thy Fathers? Thy family grew like an oak on the mountains, which meeteth the wind with its lofty head. But now it is torn from the earth. Who shall supply the place of Connal?

Here was the din of arms; and here the groans of the dying. Mournful are the wars of Fingal! O Connal! it was here thou didst fall. Thine arm was like a storm; thy sword, a beam of the sky; thy height, a rock on the plain; thine eyes, a furnace of fire. Louder than a storm was thy voice, when thou confoundest the field. Warriors fell by thy sword, as the thistle by the staff of a boy.

Dargo the mighty came on, like a cloud of thunder. His brows were contracted and dark. His eyes like two caves in a rock. Bright rose their swords on each side; dire was the clang of their steel.

The daughter of Rinval was near; Crimora, bright in the armour of man; her hair loose behind, her bow in her hand. She followed the youth to the war, Connal her much-beloved. She drew the string on Dargo; but erring pierced her Connal. He falls like an oak on the plain; like a rock from the shaggy hill. What shall she do, hapless maid! He bleeds; her Connal dies. All the night long she cries, and all the day, O Connal, my love and my friend! With grief the sad mourner died.

Earth here incloseth the loveliest pair on the hill. The grass grows between the stones of their tomb; I sit in the mournful shade. The wind sighs through the grass; and their memory rushes on my mind. Undisturbed you now sleep together; in the tomb of the mountain you rest alone.

IRISH

translated by JAMES MACPHERSON

Bran

Wounded full sore is Bran the knight;
For he was at Kerloan fight;
At Kerloan fight, by wild seashore
Was Bran-Vor's grandson wounded sore;
And, though we gained the victory,
Was captive borne beyond the sea.

He when he came beyond the sea,
In the close keep wept bitterly.
"They leap at home with joyous cry
While, woe is me, in bed I lie.
Could I but find a messenger,
Who to my mother news would bear!"

They quickly found a messenger;
His hest thus gave the warrior:
"Heed thou to dress in other guise,
My messenger, dress beggar-wise!
Take thou my ring, my ring of gold,
That she thy news as truth may hold!
Unto my country straightway go,
It to my lady mother show!
Should she come free her son from hold,
A flag of white do thou unfold!
But if with thee she come not back,
Unfurl, ah me, a pennon black!"

So, when to Leon-land he came,
At supper table sat the dame,
At table with her family,
The harpers playing as should be.
"Dame of the castle, hail! I bring
From Bran your son this golden ring,
His golden ring and letter too;
Read it, oh read it, straightway through!"

"Ye harpers, cease ye, play no more,
For with great grief my heart is sore!
      My son (cease harpers, play no more!)
In prison, and I did not know!
      Prepare to-night a ship for me!
To-morrow I go across the sea."

      The morning of the next, next day
The Lord Bran question'd, as he lay:
      "Sentinel, sentinel, soothly say!
Seest thou no vessel on its way?"
      "My lord the knight, I nought espy
Except the great sea and the sky."
      The Lord Bran askt him yet once more,
Whenas the day's course half was o'er;
      "Sentinel, sentinel, soothly say!
Seest thou no vessel on its way?"
      "I can see nothing, my lord the knight,
Except the sea-birds i' their flight."
      The Lord Bran askt him yet again,
Whenas the day was on the wane;
      "Sentinel, sentinel, soothly say!
Seest thou no vessel on its way?"
      Then that false sentinel, the while
Smiling a mischief-working smile;
      "I see afar a misty form –
A ship sore beaten by the storm."
      "The flag? Quick give the answer back!
The banner? Is it white or black?"
      "Far as I see, 'tis black, Sir knight,
I swear it by the coal's red light."
      When this the sorrowing knight had heard
Again he never spoke a word;
      But turn'd aside his visage wan;
And then the fever fit began.

Now of the townsmen askt the dame,
When at the last to shore she came,
　　"What is the news here, townsmen, tell!
That thus I hear them toll the bell?"

　　An aged man the lady heard,
And thus he answer'd to her word:
　　"We in the prison held a knight;
And he hath died here in the night."

　　Scarcely to end his words were brought,
When the high tower that lady sought;
　　Shedding salt tears and running fast,
Her white hair scatter'd in the blast,

　　So that the townsmen wonderingly
Full sorely marvell'd her to see;
　　Whenas they saw a lady strange,
Through their streets so sadly range

　　Each one in thought did musing stand;
"Who is the lady, from what land?"
　　Soon as the donjon's foot she reacht,
The porter that poor dame beseecht;

　　"Ope, quickly ope, the gate for me!
My son! My son! Him would I see!"
　　Slowly the great gate open drew;
Herself upon her son she threw,

　　Close in her arms his corpse to strain,
The lady never rose again.

　　There is a tree, that doth look o'er
From Kerloan's battle-field to th' shore;
　　An oak. Before great Evan's face
The Saxons fled in that same place.

　　Upon that oak in clear moonlight,
Together come the birds at night;
　　Black birds and white, but sea birds all;
On each one's brow a blood-stain small,

　　With them a raven gray and old;
With her a crow comes young and bold.

Both with soil'd wings, both wearied are;
They come beyond the seas from far:
And the birds sing so lovelily
That silence comes on the great sea.
All sing in concert sweet and low
Except the raven and the crow.
Once was the crow heard murmuring:
"Sing, little birds, ye well may sing!
Sing, for this is your own countrie!
Ye died not far from Brittany!"

BRETON
translated by F.G. FLEAY

from The Banquet of Dun na n-Gedh

That is good, ye men of Alba!
    What cause has brought you together?
    What object occupies your attention,
    As ye are all this day in one place?
As Erin of many adventures
    Is not your native land,
    Alas for those who go, by change of journey,
    To fight with the king of Tara.
A fair grey man of fame will meet them,
    Whose deeds are celebrated;
    He cannot be avoided, east or west,
    He will bring slaughter on the Albanachs.

O host of many a youth and steed!
    The son of Aedh, son of Ainmire.
    Through the truth of his judgment, – no falsehood,–
    Is protected by Christ.
Alas for those who shun not the plain,
    To which ye go *only* to be dispersed;
    The Gaels shall be in groups beneath the mound;
    Ye are going, but better it were to stay.
Alas for those who shun not the vale,
    Ye shall be defeated in the land of Erin;
    Not one of you shall carry his head,
    But shall sell it to the king of Erin.
Ten hundred heads shall be the beginning of your slaughter.
    Around the great fair king of Ulster,
    This number shall be slaughtered of the men of Alba.
    And ten hundred fully.
Wolves and flocks of ravens
    Shall devour the heads of your heroes.
    Until the fine clean sand is reckoned
    The heads of the Ultonians shall not be reckoned.
But prophecy is of no avail indeed
    When the obstinate are on the brink of destruction!
    Your men shall be separated from sovereignty,
    Your women shall be without constant goodness.

IRISH (12th century)
translated by JOHN O'DONOVAN

DEATH

THE LAST CEREMONY

A death touched the whole community and was a shared event in the life of the people, and with the dangerous occupations of fishing and mining it was a very real and constant threat. Death is accepted as being inevitable, and is of immediate concern to all involved in the rite of passage. Although the finality of death is recognized and there is no attempt to disguise its harsh reality, it is seen as a gateway and a release from the body to a new and richer world. We are called to 'wear those lovely colours' and to know that even in the sorrow and mourning there is the promise of hope and new life: 'May the bright land of heaven now be his home'.

from The Elegy For Llewelyn Ap Gruffydd

My heart is cold with fear in my breast.
> I grieve for the king, the oak of Aberffraw.

Pure gold he gave us with his hand,
Rightly he wore a golden diadem.
Gold cups of a golden king bring me no joy
> Of Llewelyn; no more can I wear fine arms.

Woe for my Lord, the perfect falcon,
> Woe the disaster of his fall.

Woe for the loss, woe for his fate,
> Woe that I heard how he was hurt.

***

Mine now to curse the English who robbed me,
> Mine now the need to bewail his death,

Mine to speak hardly with God, who took him
> And left me without him.

Mine now to praise him, never stinting.
Mine to remember him ever more.
The rest of my life I shall grieve for him,
> And, as I grieve, so shall I weep.

***

My heart is cold with fear in my breast.
My joy shrivels up as a stick goes dry.
Do you not see the force of the wind and rain?
Do you not see the oak-branches driven together?
Do you not see the sea biting into the land?
> Do you not see the truth preparing?

Do you not see the sun rush through the sky?
> Do you not see that the stars have fallen?

Have you no faith in God, foolish people?
> Do you not see that the world is in danger?

A prayer to you, God – let the sea flood over the land.
> Why are we left behind?

> There is no place to hide from fear,

No place to live – woe to the living!
There is no counsel, no lock, no entry,
No way to escape from the counsel of fear.
Every war-band was loyal to him,
And every warrior stood beside him,
Every strong man swore by his hand,
Every ruler and land was his.
Now every region and town is troubled,
Every household and family ruined.
All the weak, all the strong his hand protected.
Each child that lies in its cradle weeps.
It did me no good that I was tricked
Into keeping my head when he lost his.
When his head fell, terror was welcome.
When his head fell, it was good to despair.
A soldier's head, a head of glory,
Head of a chief, a leader's head.
Fair head of Llewelyn, it shocks the world
That an iron pole has transfixed it now.
Head of my lord, dread pain afflicts me,
Head of my soul, a head without speech,
Head, once honoured in nine hundred lands
And praised at nine hundred feasts.
Head of a king whose hand bore iron,
Head of a king-hawk, breaching the battle-line,
Head of a king-like wolf in the battle,
May the king of heaven care for him now!
A great lord, he had a host with him
Ready to travel to Brittany.
The true royal king of Aberffraw,
May the bright land of heaven now be his home.

OWAIN AB YR YNAD GOCH (13th century)

151

Kirkyard

A silent conquering army,
The island dead,
Column on column, each with a stone banner
Raised over his head.

A green wave full of fish
Drifted far
In wavering westering ebb-drawn shoals beyond
Sinker or star.

A labyrinth of celled
And waxen pain.
Yet I come to the honeycomb often, to sip the finished
Fragrance of men.

GEORGE MACKAY BROWN (1921–96)

The Flowers of May

IN THE DISTRICTS OF CORNOUAILLE AND ABOUT
VANNES THEY HAVE A PRETTY FUNERAL
TRADITION OF COVERING WITH FLOWERS THE
BIERS OF YOUNG GIRLS WHO DIE IN THE MONTH
OF MAY. THIS CUSTOM WAS ALSO PRESERVED IN
SOUTH WALES.

I

On the sea-shore who Jeff had seen
With rosy cheeks and eyes of sheen;

Who for the pardon had seen her start,
Had felt the happier in his heart:

But he that had seen her on her bed,
Had tears of pity for her shed,

To see the sweet sick maiden laid,
Pale as a lily in summer-shade.

To her companions she said,
That sat beside her on her bed:

"My friends, if loving friends ye be,
In God's name, do not weep for me.

"You know all living death must dree;
God's own self died – died on the tree."

II

As I went for water to the spring
I heard the nightingale sweetly sing:

"The month of May is passing e'en now,
And with it the blossom on the bough.

"The happiest lot from life they bring,
The young whom death takes in the spring.

"Ev'n as the rose drops from the spray,
So youth from life doth fall away.

"Those who die ere this week is flown,
All with fresh flowers shall be strown;

"And from those flowers shall soar heaven-high,
As from the rose-cup the butterfly."

III

Jeffik! Jeffik! did you not hear
The nightingale's song so sweet and clear?

"The month of May is passing e'en now,
And with it the blossom on the bough."

When this she heard, the gentle maid,
Crosswise her two pale hands she laid:

"I will say an *Ave Marie,*
Our Ladye sweet, in honour of thee:

"That it may please our God, thy Son,
To look with pity me upon;

"That grace to pass quick me be given,
And wait for those I love in Heaven."

The *Ave Marie* was hardly said,
When gently sank her gentle head:

The pale head sank, no more to rise;
The eyelids closed upon the eyes.

Just then beyond the court-yard pale
Was heard to sing the nightingale:

"The happiest lot from life they bring,
The young whom death takes in the spring.

"Happy the young whose biers are strown
With spring-flowers, fair and freshly blown."

BRETON

translated by TOM TAYLOR

Wear Those Lovely Colours For Me
(Reflections on a Celtic Way of Death)

Wear those lovely colours for me
    Don't wear black at all;
I do not want a sombre note
    Crossing Heaven's Hall.

No stentorian tone of organ
    Or ponderous undertaker's tread,
Or grief in my leaving
    Darken the road ahead.

Laughter with my mourning be,
    Lively make my passing here
Wear clothes of colour
    As you carry my funeral bier.

I want those lovely colours,
    Wear those clothes with pride
For I'll my finest raiment wear
    As my God I stand beside!

DONNELLY MCCORMICK (b. 1936)

Death of an Old Woman

She lived too much alone to be aware of it,
in a cottage on a stretch of moor,
built before the distant road was built
and shunned by everything built since.
Her croft had faded through the years
for lack of drainage and proper food,
bled of its green until the eye
could hardly tell where it began or ended.
Her house had a hole in the thatch
to let the smoke out – when there was any –
and the rain in, and three small openings
in the walls, two for light and one for charity,
and all about the size she was accustomed to.
The man who found her dead was drawn
in that direction by the movement.
That was the door of her empty henhouse
flapping in the wind, a nerve continuing to twitch.
She herself was lying in her bed,
causing a slight ripple in the blankets.
She had an English Bible in her hands,
upside down. The doctor who examined her
stated that her mouth was full of raw potato.

ALASDAIR MACLEAN (b. 1926)

Burial Path

When we carried you, Siân, that winter day,
over four rivers and four mountains
to the burial place of your people,
it was not the dark rocks of Cwm-y-Benglog
dragged down my spirit,
it was not the steepness of Rhiw'r Ych
that cracked my heart.

Four by four, Siân, we carried you,
over the mountain wilderness of Dewi,
fording Pysgotwr and Doithïe,
crossing Camddwr by Soar-y-Mynydd,
Tywi at Nant-y-Neuadd; every river passed
brought us the challenge of another hill beyond.

Again and again from his rough pony's back our leader
signalled with his hazel-staff of office
four, breathless, to lay down your coffin,
four, fresh in strength, to bear you
up the old sledge-ways, the sinew-straining tracks,
the steeps of Rhiw Gelynen and Rhiw'r Ych.

I with the rest, Siân, carried you.
The burial path is long – forty times and more
I put my shoulder to the coffin
before the weary journey was accomplished
and down at last through leafless oaks
singing we carried you to the crumbling church,
the ancient yews, at the burial place of your people.

It was not then my heart cracked, Siân,
nor my soul went into darkness.
Carrying you, there was great weariness,
and pride in an old ritual well performed –
our friend's firm leadership, smooth changes

from four to four, the coffin riding
effortlessly the surge of effort.
And at the grave, pride too in showing
churchmen how we of Soar knew well
ways of devotion, fit solemnity.

But with your grave whitened – the last ceremony –
and my neighbours, as I had urged them, gone ahead,
then it was I felt the weight of death
for the first time, Siân, and I knew
it would be always with me now
on the bitter journey that was not yet accomplished.

Now as I went down Rhiw'r Ych alone
and turned west over the ford of Nant-y-Neuadd,
I knew there was only darkness waiting
for me, beyond the crags of Cwm-y-Benglog.
It was then my heart cracked, Siân, my spirit
went into that darkness and was lost.

RUTH BIDGOOD (b. 1922)

OTHERWORLD

DREAMS GATHER

The Otherworld: a place of mystery, of miraculous visions, a dreamworld of shape-shifting and magic, where Monann could change from a wolf to a stag to a salmon, a dangerous world of faery where nothing was certain. Here a child might be lured away or Mael Dúin meet a beautiful woman with golden hair and silver shoes. Another version of this marvellous world was to be found beyond the sea and setting sun to the west, The Isles of the Blessed, that one journeyed to after death and where all wishes could be fulfilled. It was 'a way to the gate of glory' for the Christian Celt where he would be united with Christ and his people. For the Celt this spirit world also suffused and penetrated our known world of the senses, and in an instant would transform it 'to a brightness that seemed as transitory as your youth once, but is the eternity that awaits you'.

from Iona: Bride

But when the middle of the year came that was (though Dùvach had forgotten it) the year of the prophecy, his eldest son, Conn, who was now a man, murmured against the virginity of Bride, because of her beauty and because a chieftain of the mainland was eager to wed her. 'I shall wed Bride or raid Iona,' was the message he had sent.

So one day, before the Great Fire of the Summer Festival, Conn and his brothers reproached Bride.

'Idle are these pure eyes, O Bride, not to be as lamps at thy marriage-bed.'
'Truly, it is not by the eyes that we live,' replied the maiden gently, while to their fear and amazement she passed her hand before her face and let them see that the sockets were empty.

Trembling with awe at this portent, Dùvach intervened:

'By the sun I swear it, O Bride, that thou shalt marry whomsoever thou wilt and none other, and when thou wilt, or not at all, if such be thy will.'

And when he had spoken, Bride smiled, and passed her hand before her face again, and all there were abashed because of the blue light as of morning that was in her shining eyes.

It was while the dew was yet wet on the grass that on the morrow Bride came out of her father's house, and went up the steep slope of Dùn-I. The crying of the ewes and lambs at the pastures came plaintively against the dawn. The lowing of the kye arose from the sandy hollows by the shore, or from the meadows on the lower slopes. Through the whole island went a rapid, trickling sound, most sweet to hear: the myriad voices of twittering birds, from the dotterel in the seaweed, to the larks climbing the blue slopes of heaven.

This was the festival of her birth, and she was clad in white. About her waist was a girdle of the sacred rowan, the feathery green leaves flickering dusky shadows upon her robe as she moved. The light upon her yellow hair was as when morning wakes, laughing in wind amid the tall corn. As she went she sang to herself, softly as the crooning of a dove. If any had been there to hear he would have been abashed, for the words were not in Erse, and the eyes of the beautiful girl were as those of one in a vision.

FIONA MACLEOD (1855–1905)

The Valley of the Black Pig

The dews drop slowly and dreams gather: unknown spears
Suddenly hurtle before my dream-awakened eyes,
And then the clash of fallen horsemen and the cries
Of unknown perishing armies beat about my ears.
We who still labour by the cromlech on the shore,
The grey cairn on the hill, when day sinks drowned in dew,
Being weary of the world's empires, bow down to you,
Master of the still stars and of the flaming door.

W.B. YEATS (1865–1939)

The Deer's Cry

I arise to-day
Through a mighty strength, the
   invocation of the Trinity,
Through belief in the threeness,
Through confession of the oneness
Of the Creator of Creation.

I arise to-day
Through the strength of Christ's birth
   with His baptism,
Through the strength of His crucifixion
   with His burial,
Through the strength of His resurrection
   with His ascension,
Through the strength of His descent for
   the judgment of Doom.

I arise to-day
Through the strength of the love of
   Cherubim,
In obedience of angels,
In the service of archangels,
In hope of resurrection to meet with
   reward,
In prayers of patriarchs,
In predictions of prophets,
In preachings of apostles,
In faiths of confessors,
In innocence of holy virgins,
In deeds of righteous men.

I arise to-day
Through the strength of heaven:
Light of sun,
Radiance of moon,

Splendour of fire,
Speed of lightning,
Swiftness of wind,
Depth of sea,
Stability of earth,
Firmness of rock.

I arise to-day
Through God's strength to pilot me:
God's might to uphold me,
God's wisdom to guide me,
God's eye to look before me,
God's ear to hear me,
God's word to speak for me,
God's hand to guard me,
God's way to lie before me,
God's shield to protect me,
God's host to save me
From snares of devils,
From temptations of vices,
From every one who shall wish me ill,
Afar and anear,
Alone and in a multitude.

I summon to-day all these powers
    between me and those evils,
Against every cruel merciless power that
    may oppose my body and soul,
Against incantations of false prophets,
Against black laws of pagandom,
Against false laws of heretics,
Against craft of idolatry,
Against spells of women and smiths and
    wizards,
Against every knowledge that corrupts
    man's body and soul.

Christ to shield me to-day
Against poison, against burning,
Against drowning, against wounding,
So that there may come to me abundance
    of reward.
Christ with me, Christ before me, Christ
    behind me,
Christ in me, Christ beneath me, Christ
    above me,
Christ on my right, Christ on my left,
Christ when I lie down, Christ when I sit
    down, Christ when I arise,
Christ in the heart of every man who
    thinks of me,
Christ in the mouth of every one who
    speaks of me,
Christ in every eye that sees me,
Christ in every ear that hears me.

I arise to-day
Through a mighty strength, the
    invocation of the Trinity,
Through belief in the threeness,
Through confession of the oneness
Of the Creator of Creation.

IRISH

translated by KUNO MEYER

Maytime Thoughts

Maytime is the nicest time,
birds are loud,
trees are green;
ploughs are in the furrow,
oxen in the yoke.
The sea is green,
lands have many colours.

When cuckoos sing
on the tops of fine trees,
sadness
grows.

Smoke stings,
at night I'm all too restless
since my loved ones
have gone to the grave.

On hill,
in hollow,
on islands in the sea,
everywhere you go
before blessed Christ
there is no place that is God-forsaken.

In desire,
in lust,
in transgression,
it is time
to make for
the land of your final retreat.
Seven saints,
seven score,
seven hundred
gone in one convocation:
with Christ the blessed
dread
they do not suffer.

A boon I ask,
may you not refuse me:
let there be peace
between God and me.
Let there be for me
a way to the gate of glory.
Amongst your people
Christ
I mayn't be sad.

WELSH (13th century)

translated by MEIRION PENNAR

from The Voyage of Mael Dúin

Then on the fourth day the woman came to them, and in a lovely guise she came. A white cloak round her, and a circlet of gold round her hair. Her hair was golden. Two silver shoes on her pink and white feet. A silver brooch with golden filigree in her cloak, and a filmy robe of silk next to her white body. 'Welcome, Mael Dúin,' she said, and she called every man in turn by his own proper name. 'For a long time your coming here has been known and accepted,' she said. Then she took them with her into a great house which was close to the sea, and had their boat pulled up on land. They saw then in the house ready for them a bed for Mael Dúin and a bed for every three of his followers. She brought them food in a hamper, like cheese or sour buttermilk, and she gave out helpings for three at a time. Each man found in it whatever taste he desired. Then she served Mael Dúin by himself. She filled a bucket beneath the same plank, and poured drink for them. She made a trip for every three men in turn. She saw when they had had enough, and ceased pouring for them. 'A woman fit for Mael Dúin is this woman,' said every man of his followers. After that she left them, with her hamper and her bucket. His men said to Mael Dúin, 'Shall we speak to her to ask whether she would sleep with you?' 'What harm would it do you,' said he, 'if you speak to her?' She came the next day at the same time to serve them, as she did before. They said to the girl, 'Will you make a match with Mael Dúin, and sleep with him? Why not stay here tonight?' She said that she had not learned and did not know what sin was. Then she went away to her house, and came the next day at the same time with her service for them. When they were surfeited and drunk, they said the same words to her. 'Tomorrow then,' said she, 'you shall be given an answer about this.' She went after that to her house, and they fell asleep on their beds. When they awoke, they were in their boat on a rock, and they did not see the island nor the fortress nor the woman nor the place where they were before...

IRISH (8th–9th century)
translated by K.H. JACKSON

The Bright Field

I have seen the sun break through
to illuminate a small field
for a while, and gone my way
and forgotten it. But that was the pearl
of great price, the one field that had
the treasure in it. I realise now
that I must give all that I have
to possess it. Life is not hurrying

on to a receding future, nor hankering after
an imagined past. It is the turning
aside like Moses to the miracle
of the lit bush, to a brightness
that seemed as transitory as your youth
once, but is the eternity that awaits you.

R.S. THOMAS (b. 1913)

from The Secret Commonwealth of Elves, Fauns and Fairies

Their apparel and speech is like that of the people and country under which they live: so they are seen to wear plaids and variegated garments in the Highlands of Scotland and Suanochs (*sunach* or tartan) heretofore in Ireland. They speak but little, and that by way of whistling, clear, not rough. The very devils conjured in any country do answer in the language of that place, yet sometimes these subterraneans do speak more distinctly than at other times.

Their women are said to spin, very finely, to dye, to tissue and embroider; but whether it be as [a] manual operation of substantial refined stuffs with apt and solid instruments, or only curious cobwebs, impalpable rainbows, and a fantastic imitation of the actions of more terrestrial mortals, since it transcended all the senses of the seer to discern whither, I leave to conjecture, [just] as I found it.

ROBERT KIRK (1644–97)

translated by R.J. STEWART

The Stolen Child

Where dips the rocky highland
Of Sleuth Wood in the lake,
There lies a leafy island
Where flapping herons wake
The drowsy water-rats;
There we've hid our faery vats,
Full of berries
And of reddest stolen cherries.
Come away, O human child!
To the waters and the wild
With a faery, hand in hand,
For the world's more full of weeping than
    you can understand.

Where the wave of moonlight glosses
The dim grey sands with light,
Far off by furthest Rosses
We foot it all the night,
Weaving olden dances,
Mingling hands and mingling glances
Till the moon has taken flight;
To and fro we leap
And chase the frothy bubbles,
While the world is full of troubles
And is anxious in its sleep.
Come away, O human child!
To the waters and the wild
With a faery, hand in hand,
For the world's more full of weeping than
    you can understand.

Where the wandering water gushes
From the hills above Glen-Car,
In pools among the rushes
That scarce could bathe a star,

We seek for slumbering trout
And whispering in their ears
Give them unquiet dreams;
Leaning softly out
From ferns that drop their tears
Over the young streams.
Come away, O human child!
To the waters and the wild
With a faery, hand in hand,
For the world's more full of weeping than
  you can understand.

Away with us he's going,
The solemn-eyed:
He'll hear no more the lowing
Of the calves on the warm hillside
Or the kettle on the hob
Sing peace into his breast,
Or see the brown mice bob
Round and round the oatmeal-chest.
For he comes, the human child,
To the waters and the wild
With a faery, hand in hand,
From a world more full of weeping than
  he can understand.

W.B. YEATS (1865–1939)

from The Voyage of Bran

Then on the morrow Bran went upon the sea. The number of his men was three companies of nine. One of his foster-brothers and mates was set over each of the three companies of nine. When he had been at sea two days and two nights, he saw a man in a chariot coming towards him over the sea. That man also sang thirty other quatrains to him, and made himself known to him, and said that he was Manannan the son of Ler, and said that it was upon him to go to Ireland after long ages, and that a son would be born to him, even Mongan son of Fiachna – that was the name which would be upon him.

So he sang these thirty quatrains to him:

> Bran deems it a marvellous beauty
> In his coracle across the clear sea:
> While to me in my chariot from afar
> It is a flowery plain on which he rides about.
>
> What is a clear sea
> For the prowed skiff in which Bran is,
> That is a happy plain with profusion of flowers
> To me from the chariot of two wheels.
>
> Bran sees
> The number of waves beating across the clear sea:
> I myself see in Mag Mon
> Red-headed flowers without fault.
>
> Sea-horses glisten in summer
> As far as Bran has stretched his glance:
> Rivers pour forth a stream of honey
> In the land of Manannan son of Ler.
>
> The sheen of the main, on which thou art,
> The white hue of the sea on which thou rowest about,
> Yellow and azure are spread out,
> It is land, and is not rough.

Speckled salmon leap from the womb
Of the white sea, on which thou lookest:
They are calves, they are coloured lambs
With friendliness, without mutual slaughter.

Though [but] one chariot-rider is seen
In Mag Mell of many flowers,
There are many steeds on its surface,
Though them thou seest not.

The size of the plain, the number of the host,
Colours glisten with pure glory,
A fair stream of silver, cloths of gold,
Afford a welcome with all abundance.

A beautiful game, most delightful,
They play [sitting] at the luxurious wine,
Men and gentle women under a bush,
Without sin, without crime.

Along the top of a wood has swum
Thy coracle across ridges,
There is a wood of beautiful fruit
Under the prow of thy little skiff.

A wood with blossom and fruit,
On which is the vine's veritable fragrance,
A wood without decay, without defect,
On which are leaves of golden hue.

We are from the beginning of creation
Without old age, without consummation of earth,
Hence we expect not that there should be frailty,
The sin has not come to us.

An evil day when the Serpent went
To the father to his city!
She has perverted the times in this world,
So that there came decay which was not original.

By greed and lust he has slain us,
Through which he has ruined his noble race:
The withered body has gone to the fold of torment,
And everlasting abode of torture.

It is a law of pride in this world
To believe in the creatures, to forget God,
Overthrow by diseases, and old age,
Destruction of the soul through deception.

A noble salvation will come
From the King who has created us,
A white law will come over seas,
Besides being God, He will be man.

This shape, he on whom thou lookest,
Will come to thy parts;
'Tis mine to journey to her house,
To the woman in Line-mag.

For it is Moninnan, the son of Ler,
From the chariot in the shape of a man,
Of his progeny will be a very short while
A fair man in a body of white clay.

Monann, the descendant of Ler, will be
A vigorous bed-fellow to Caintigern:
He shall be called to his son in the beautiful world,
Fiachna will acknowledge him as his son.

He will delight the company of every fairy-knoll,
He will be the darling of every goodly land,
He will make known secrets – a course of wisdom –
In the world, without being feared.

He will be in the shape of every beast,
Both on the azure sea and on land,
He will be a dragon before hosts at the onset,
He will be a wolf of every great forest.

He will be a stag with horns of silver
In the land where chariots are driven,
He will be a speckled salmon in a full pool,
He will be a seal, he will be a fair-white swan.

He will be throughout long ages
An hundred years in fair kingship,
He will cut down battalions, – a lasting grave –
He will redden fields, a wheel around the track.

It will be about kings with a champion
That he will be known as a valiant hero,
Into the stronghold of a land on a height
I shall send an appointed end from Islay.

High shall I place him with princes,
He will be overcome by a son of error;
Moninnan, the son of Ler,
Will be his father, his tutor.

He will be – his time will be short –
Fifty years in this world:
A dragonstone from the sea will kill him
In the fight at Senlabor.

He will ask a drink from Loch Ló,
While he looks at the stream of blood,
The white host will take him under a wheel of clouds
To the gathering where there is no sorrow.

Steadily then let Bran row,
Not far to the Land of Women,
Emne with many hues of hospitality
Thou wilt reach before the setting of the sun.

IRISH

translated by KUNO MEYER

from Iona: Dûn-I

As I write, here on the hill-slope of Dun-I, the sound
of the furtive wave is as the sighing in a shell. I am
alone between sea and sky, for there is no other on
this bouldered height, nothing visible but a single
blue shadow that slowly sails the hillside. The bleat-
ing of lambs and ewes, the lowing of kine, these come
up from the Machar that lies between the west slopes
and the shoreless sea to the west; these ascend as the
very smoke of sound. All round the island there is a
continuous breathing; deeper and more prolonged on
the west, where the open sea is; but audible everywhere. The seals on Soa are even now putting their
breasts against the running tide; for I see a flashing of
fins here and there in patches at the north end of the
Sound, and already from the ruddy granite shores of
the Ross there is a congregation of seafowl – gannets
and guillemots, skuas and herring-gulls, the long-
necked northern diver, the tern, the cormorant. In the
sunblaze, the waters of the Sound dance their blue
bodies and swirl their flashing white hair o' foam;
and, as I look, they seem to me like children of the
wind and the sunshine, leaping and running in these
flowing pastures, with a laughter as sweet against the
ears as the voices of children at play.

The joy of life vibrates everywhere. Yet the Weaver
does not sleep, but only dreams. He loves the sun-
drowned shadows. They are invisible thus, but they
are there, in the sunlight itself. Sure, they may be
heard: as, an hour ago, when on my way hither by the
Stairway of the Kings – for so sometimes they call
here the ancient stones of the mouldered princes of
long ago – I heard a mother moaning because of the
son that had had to go over-sea and leave her in her
old age; and heard also a child sobbing, because of the

sorrow of childhood – that sorrow so unfathomable, so incommunicable. And yet not a stone's-throw from where I lie, half hidden beneath an overhanging rock, is the Pool of Healing. To this small, black-brown tarn, pilgrims of every generation, for hundreds of years, have come. Solitary, these; not only because the pilgrim to the Fount of Eternal Youth must fare hither alone, and at dawn, so as to touch the healing water the moment the first sunray quickens it – but solitary, also, because those who go in quest of this Fount of Youth are the dreamers and the Children of Dream, and these are not many, and few come now to this lonely place. Yet, an Isle of Dream Iona is, indeed. Here the last sun-worshippers bowed before the Rising of God; here Columba and his hymning priests laboured and brooded; and here Oran or his kin dreamed beneath the monkish cowl that pagan dream of his. Here, too, the eyes of Fionn and Oisìn, and of many another of the heroic men and women of the Fiànna, may have lingered; here the Pict and the Celt bowed beneath the yoke of the Norse pirate, who, too, left his dreams, or rather his strangely beautiful soul-rainbows, as a heritage to the stricken; here, for century after century, the Gael has lived, suffered, joyed, dreamed his impossible, beautiful dream; as here, now, he still lives, still suffers patiently, still dreams, and through all and over all, broods upon the incalculable mysteries. He is an elemental, among the elemental forces. He knows the voices of wind and sea: and it is because the Fount of Youth upon Dun-I of Iona is not the only wellspring of peace, that the Gael can front destiny as he does, and can endure. Who knows where its tributaries are? They may be in your heart, or in mine, and in a myriad others.

I would that the birds of Angus Òg might, for once, be changed, not, as fabled, into the kisses of love, but into doves of peace, that they might fly into the green world, and nest there in many hearts, in many minds, crooning their incommunicable song of joy and hope.

A doomed and passing race. I have been taken to task for these words. But they are true, in the deep reality where they obtain. Yes, but true only in one sense, however vital that is. The Breton's eyes are slowly turning from the enchanted West, and slowly his ears are forgetting the whisper of the wind around menhir and dolmen. The Manxman has ever been the mere yeoman of the Celtic chivalry; but even his rude dialect perishes year by year. In Wales, a great tradition survives; in Ireland, a supreme tradition fades through sunset-hued horizons; in Celtic Scotland, a passionate regret, a despairing love and longing, narrows yearly before a dull and incredibly selfish alienism. The Celt has at last reached his horizon. There is no shore beyond. He knows it. This has been the burden of his song since Malvina led the blind Oisìn to his grave by the sea: "Even the Children of Light must go down into darkness." But this apparition of a passing race is no more than the fulfilment of a glorious resurrection before our very eyes. For the genius of the Celtic race stands out now with averted torch, and the light of it is a glory before the eyes, and the flame of it is blown into the hearts of the stronger people. The Celt fades, but his spirit rises in the heart and the mind of the Anglo-Celtic peoples, with whom are the destinies of generations to come.

FIONA MACLEOD (1855–1905)

The Return of Taliesin

On my lips the speech, in my ears the sound of the Armorican:
I hear the voice of Esus by the shores of the ocean,
And the songs which the great bard Ossian
    Resings by the ancient dolmen.

Many times since this, my twelfth rebirth on earth,
Have I seen the mistletoe grow green on the oak,
Seen the yellow crocus, the sunbright, and the vervein
    Bloom again in the woodlands:

But never shall I see again the white-robed Druid of old
Seek the sacred mistletoe as one seeketh a treasure;
Never more shall I see him cut the living plant
    With his golden sickle.

Alas! the valiant chiefs with the flowing locks!
All sleep in the cairns, beneath the fresh green grass;
In vain my voice o'er the fields of the dead lamenting –
    "Vengeance! Treason!

"Be swift, Revenge, on the feet of the sorrows of Arvor!"
Alas, dull echoes alone answer my wailing summons.
Treason, indeed, and Vengeance! for lo, in the hallowed Némèdes
    The wayside flaunt of the Cross!

Tarann no longer sends forth his terror of thunder!
Camul no longer laughs behind the strength of his arm!
Tentatès, rising in wrath, has not yet crumbled the earth;
  Esus is deaf to our call!

Whither, O whither fled are ye, ye powerful, redoubtable gods;
And ye, ye famous Druids, the glory and terror of Armor?
Who has usurped, who has o'erwhelmed ye, unconquerable knights,
  Warriors of the golden collar?

Thou, who harkenest, I have been in the place of the Ancients!
I, alone among mortals, thence have issued alive:
Alas, the temple was deserted: I saw nought but some wind-haunted oaks
  Swaying in the silence.

All is fugitive! pride, pleasure, the song, the dance,
Blithe joys of friendship, noble rivalries all:
The keen swift song of the swords, the whistling lances!
  Dreams of a dreamer all! … But no,

A new dawn wakes and laughs on the breast of the darkness;
Earth has her sunshine still, the grave her Spring:
Many a time Dylan hath oared me afar in the death-barque,
  Many a death-sleep mine, and long!

For long I have slept with the heavy sleep of the dead,
Ofttimes my fugitive body has passed into divers forms,
I have spread strong wings on the air, I have swum in dark waters,
  I have crawled in the woods.

But, amid all these manifold changes, my soul
Remaineth ever the same: it is always, always "myself"!
And now I see well that this is the law of all that liveth,
  Though none beholdeth the reason, none the end.

Still stand our lonely menhirs, and still the wayfarer shudders
As in the desolate dusk he passes these Stones of Silence!
Thou speakest, I understand! Thy Breton tongue
  Is that of the ancient Kymry.

Lights steal through the hours of shadow flame-lit for unknown saints,
As, in the days of old, our torches flared on the night:
Ah, before ever these sacred lamps shone for your meek apostles,
      They burned for Héol.

Blind without reason are we, thus changing the names of the gods:
Thus, mayhap, we think to destroy them, we who abandon their altars!
But, cold, calm, unsmiling before our laughter and curses,
      The gods wait, immortal.

Yea, while the sacred fires still burn along the hill-tops,
Yea, while a single lichened menhir still looms from the brushwood,
Yea, whether they name thee Armorica, Brittany, Breiz-Izèl,
      Thou art ever the same dear land!

Ah, soul of me ofttimes to thee, Land of mystery!
Ofttimes again shall I breathe in thy charmed air!
Sure, every weary singer knoweth the secret name of thee,
      Land of Heart's Desire!

Enduring thou art! For not the slow frost of the ages
Shall dim from thy past thy glory immortally graven! –
Granite thy soil, thy soul, loved nest of Celtic nations! –
      Sings the lost Voice, Taliesin.

LEO-KERMORVAN (19th century)

186

The Soul

❊

Soul, since I was made in necessity blameless
True it is, woe is me that thou shouldst have come to my design,
Neither for my own sake, nor for death, nor for end, nor for beginning.
It was with seven faculties that I was thus blessed,
With seven created beings I was placed for purification;
I was gleaming fire when I was caused to exist;
I was dust of the earth, and grief could not reach me;
I was a high wind, being less evil than good;
I was a mist on a mountain seeking supplies of stags;
I was blossoms of trees on the face of the earth.
If the Lord had blessed me, He would have placed me on matter.
      Soul, since I was made –

WELSH

from THE BLACK BOOK OF CARMARTHEN

INDEX OF POETS AND TRANSLATORS

INDEX OF FIRST LINES